LONDON
Like a Local

BY THE PEOPLE WHO CALL IT HOME

Contents

NIGHTLIFE

OUTDOORS

meet the locals

FLORENCE DERRICK

Florence moved to London to kick-start her career in journalism. Though her writing takes her all over the world, it's East London that she knows like the back of her hand. Outside of eating, drinking and dancing – in the name of journalism – Florence is sipping flat whites, browsing charity shops and researching gig tickets.

MARLENE LANDU

Regulatory advisor Marlene settled in London in the 2000s and doesn't plan on leaving any time soon. The old 9–5 job aside, she loves to practise her downward dog, amble along Broadway Market and dish out restaurant recommendations to her friends (she seriously knows her stuff).

OLIVIA PASS

Born in London, Olivia spent her early years in Hong Kong, which gave her a lifelong travel bug. When she's not working as a photographer and writer, Olivia is cycling between bakeries in search of London's perfect brownie, rambling through Dulwich Park with her husband and dog or enjoying a wild swim.

London

WELCOME TO THE CITY

There are countless types of Londoner: long-time market traders whose roots run deep; recent graduates lured by the buzz; generations of immigrants who've breathed new life into the city. Yet what unites them all is the fact that – first and foremost – they are Londoners. Yes, they moan about overcrowded Tubes and eye-watering rent, but deep down they know that their home is like no other. It's a place with a fierce spirit, an engrained Blitz-like mentality that keeps soldiering on. Start-ups have sprouted in cracks caused by financial crisis, peaceful protests have given voice to all and communities have pulled together through thick and thin.

Think of London and you'll probably picture its iconic façade: majestic bridges lacing the Thames, the riverbanks sown with gleaming skyscrapers and historic landmarks. But famous sights aside, London is, at its core, a place where people live – a tapestry of distinctive neighbourhoods, woven with Victorian terraces and tower blocks, and punctuated by well-trodden parks and beloved boozers. It's in these neighbourhood communities that London is at its most real, and its most exciting.

And that's exactly where this book comes in. We know the places that Londoners love, from just whispered-about restaurants to underground venues that nurture old and new talent. Of course, with nearly 9 million citizens, there are more Londoners than these pages can do justice to. Instead, this book celebrates snapshots of local life in a city that's as diverse as its inhabitants.

Whether you're a restless Londoner hungry to find the places that aren't on everyone else's radar, or a visitor looking to delve beyond the city's icons, this book will help you embrace a lesser-known London. So tear up the traditional bucket list, and enjoy London the local way.

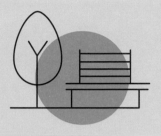

Liked by the locals

"Sure, London can be exhausting. It constantly badgers you to keep up, teasing you with the constant gamble of what to do, and what to miss. But that's what I love most about London – you can never get bored."

OLIVIA PASS,
PHOTOGRAPHER AND TRAVEL WRITER

London takes on different personalities during each of the seasons. Think jubilant festivals in summer, cosy pub lunches in autumn and festive fun in winter.

London
THROUGH THE YEAR

SPRING

RIVERSIDE EXPLORATION
As life unfurls after winter, Londoners inch outdoors to walk along the Thames path and cycle beside barge-dotted canals that snake around the city.

MARKETS GALORE
Locals embrace the milder weather by migrating to the city's outdoor markets. They gather blooms on Columbia Road (p100), guzzle snacks at Maltby Street Market (p40) and hunt for vintage treasures on Portobello Road (p85).

OUTDOOR CINEMAS
From May onwards, open-air cinemas spring up across the city. Classic films are enjoyed with blankets, deck chairs and cocktails. The most spectacular is Secret Cinema, an immersive cinematic experience held in a secret location.

SUMMER

FESTIVAL FUN
Nothing brings Londoners together like its summer festival season. Pride in July and Notting Hill Carnival in August are joyous cultural celebrations, while the abundant music festivals — All Points East, Lovebox, Wireless and South West Four, to name but a few — draw fans from all corners of the city.

WONDERFUL WIMBLEDON
Queueing at the crack of dawn for tickets to this famous tournament is a rite of passage for many locals. Those

less keen on an early wake-up call head to the big screens at Granary Square or St Katharine Docks instead.

PARKS AND PICNICS
As temperatures rise, Londoners descend on the city's parks and gardens to celebrate the warm weather. Dog walkers stop to chat, families throw frisbees and friends toast the summer.

AUTUMN

CULTURAL TOURS
With the days cooling off, Londoners head indoors for a dose of culture. The curious join guided tours around private houses as part of September's Open House Festival and enjoy events during October's Museums at Night weekend.

WEEKEND ROASTS
On a cold and rainy weekend there's one place Londoners are guaranteed to gather: a cosy pub serving slap-up roasts with all the trimmings.

FIREWORKS FOR DAYS
London's skies erupt with fireworks on Bonfire Night (5 November) and during Diwali, in mid-November. Most

weekends include a dazzling display of fireworks, sparklers and locals cocooned in coats in the city's parks.

WINTER

CHRISTMAS IN THE CITY
Festive markets and ice rinks pop up across the city, the city centre is strung with lights and mulled wine is added to pub menus. It's the same every year and yet locals still lap it all up.

JOLLY JUMPERS
Londoners love a festive jumper – the more garish, the better – and most of London's Christmas parties entail wearing a brightly patterned knit.

NEW YEAR'S EVE
While some Londoners seek a riverside spot to watch the New Year's Eve fireworks over the Thames, most prefer to watch the show on the TV with a glass of champers and their loved ones.

DRY JANUARY
Tired and broke after Christmas, Londoners often promise they won't drink in January. But a few weeks into the year and most ask their friends, "pub?"

There's an art to being a Londoner, from the dos and don'ts in the pub to negotiating the city's intricate streets. Here's a breakdown of all you need to know.

London
KNOW-HOW

For a directory of health and safety resources, safe spaces and accessibility information, turn to page 186. For everything else, read on.

EAT

Londoners will find any excuse to eat out. Weekends revolve around leisurely brunches and roasts, with restaurants and pubs starting to fill up from 11am. Dinner is the main meal of the day and starts any time from 7 or 8pm. It's a good idea to book a table wherever possible, though some hotspots don't take reservations. They'll instead ask for your number on arrival and text you when your table is ready, so you can nip off for a drink.

DRINK

Pubs are so much more than places to drink; they're social institutions. Our tips? Make sure you buy a "round" – a drink for each person in your group – and wait your turn at the bar (one of the few places that locals don't queue, but it's still polite). Last orders are around 10:45pm, when a bell is rung as a prompt before the bar closes at 11pm.

Londoners are fuelled by coffee and largely drink it from takeaway cups as they go about their day. Some cafés offer a discount if you bring a reusable cup.

SHOP

Londoners tend to avoid Oxford Street, preferring to shop on their local high streets, which have a mix of chains and independents. Shops are generally open from 9am to 5:30pm, though they often close earlier on Sundays. Markets are usually held on weekends only and, these days, haggling isn't really the done thing. It's always worth carrying a tote bag to avoid the charge for a plastic one.

ARTS & CULTURE

London's big museums and galleries are, wonderfully, free to enter, though you do need to buy tickets to temporary exhibitions. Popular theatre shows can be pricey and need to be booked well in advance but box offices do last-minute deals. Performances usually start around 7pm and round off by 11pm. It's all very casual these days so you don't need to dress up (unless you want to, of course).

NIGHTLIFE

Nights out in London generally start in the pub, or with "pre-drinks" at home, if the plan is to hit a club later. Doors open at clubs and music venues around 7pm but things don't really get started until 9 or 10pm. Lots of bars and pubs turn into dance venues around 10pm, too, with tables getting pushed to the side. When it comes to what to wear, again, you don't need to dress up. Just be sure to have your ID on you — security at the door nearly always ask, however old you look.

OUTDOORS

On a sunny day, Londoners flock to the city's parks for picnics and catch-ups. Here there are countless recycling and rubbish bins — do your bit to help look after these green spaces. There's also a big homeless population in London so be respectful of the community while in the city's parks. The canal towpaths make for a lovely stroll but note that walkers share the narrow paths with cyclists.

Keep in mind

Here are some more tips and tidbits that will help you fit in like a local.

» **Contactless** The majority of places take contactless payment, including markets, museums and the city's transport systems.

» **No smoking** If you want to smoke or vape, do so in a designated spot outside.

» **Tipping** A tip of 10 or 12.5 per cent is the norm in restaurants, with some places adding it to the bill as a matter of course.

» **Stay hydrated** London is home to lots of free drinking fountains, so bring a reusable bottle. You can also ask bartenders to refill it for you.

GETTING AROUND

London is made up of 12 inner boroughs and 20 outer boroughs, each of which comprise a handful of neighbourhoods (p14). Generally speaking, though, locals think of London both physically and culturally as five distinct areas – central, north, south, east and west, with the Thames running through the city's heart. Postcodes also reflect these areas and are included on many street signs (SW, for example, refers to neighbourhoods south and then west of central), which can help you navigate your way around the city. Most locals live outside of central London.

To make your life easier we've provided what3words addresses for each sight in this book, meaning you can quickly pinpoint exactly where you're heading with ease.

On foot

London is so well served by the Underground that it's easy to forget how walkable the city is. It's not uncommon for Londoners to get off the Tube a stop early and walk the last leg of their journey, especially if it means avoiding a notoriously crowded station (Oxford Circus: we're looking at you). Besides which, walking is the best way to see the city in all its glory. Having said this, Londoners are very fast walkers, so don't dawdle in the middle of the pavement. If you do need to stop and check a what3words location, step to the side so that people can pass.

On wheels

This is a city of keen cyclists and so the cycle lane network is constantly being improved. Hitting central London on two wheels can be a little daunting so try and stick to other cyclists if you can. Watch out for pedestrians crossing the road, never go through a red light (even if you see your fellow cyclists doing it) and try not to cycle too close to the curb – it gives drivers the impression that they can get past you, even if there's not enough room. Finally, always wear a helmet. No arguments.

Visitors can use the public bicycle scheme, Santander Cycles, which has over 750 docking stations across London. You can hire them via the official app or by using your bank card at one of the docking stations. It costs £2 to access a bike for 24 hours, with the first 30 minutes of each journey free. Note that the legal drink-drive limit (85 mg of alcohol per 100 ml of blood, equivalent to a small glass of wine or a pint of lager) also applies to cyclists. *www.santandercycles.co.uk*

By public transport

London's transport network, which is run by Transport for London (TfL), includes the Underground (or "the Tube"), buses, the Overground and Docklands Light Railway (DLR). National Rail looks after the trains running in and out of the city.

Once you've learned the basics of the Tube, it's easy to navigate. In short, Tube lines are colour-coded and trains travel in two directions: north and south, or east and west. Fares vary depending on the time of day you're travelling (a single fare ranges from £2.60 to £3.20). To pay, tap in and out of stations with an Oyster card (preloaded with money), a contactless card or your phone. Paper tickets are also available. London's red buses are ubiquitous. Payment is contactless only and pay-as-you-go; the Hopper fare gives unlimited journeys for £1.65 within one hour of tapping in.

By car or taxi

Londoners don't tend to drive. There's an off-putting daily fee of £15 for cars entering the central Congestion Zone plus awful traffic. Now and then they use taxis, like the iconic black cabs, which can be hailed on the street in central London or booked with the Gett Taxi app. For cheaper fares, they prefer the likes of Uber, Bolt and Ola.

Download these

We recommend you download these apps to help you get about the city.

WHAT3WORDS
Your geocoding friend

A what3words address is a simple way to communicate any precise location on earth, using just three words. ///pipes.actor.bossy, for example, is the code for the David Bowie mural in Brixton. Simply download the free what3words app, type a what3words address into the search bar, and you'll know exactly where to go.

TFL
Your local transport service

The app from Transport for London lays out all your best options for moving around the city, as well as live departures and delay information for each stop. It's a great source for checking when the last train or bus is, too, so you don't miss either.

London is a city of cities and every neighbourhood has its own wonderful flavour and community. Here we take a look at some of our favourites.

London

NEIGHBOURHOODS

Bermondsey

Once a centre of industry, Bermondsey is known for its enviable warehouse flats, world-class restaurant scene and craft breweries, which culminate in the Bermondsey Beer Mile. {map 5}

Bethnal Green

Old East End flavour lives on here, with stalwarts like Columbia Road Flower Market giving a window to the past. Shabby-chic spaces now house bougie bars and restaurants, tempting young professionals to put down roots in the area. {map 2}

Brixton

Historically a multiethnic area, with a strong Afro-Caribbean community, Brixton has seen contentious gentrification. Having said that, it's still hard to beat for powerful street art and buzzing markets. {map 5}

Camden

Famed for its counterculture, Camden was at the heart of the punk rock movement in the 70s, and Britpop in the mid-90s. Music lovers still journey across the city for a gig here, ideally after a few hours sat by the Regent's Canal or a bite at Camden Market. {map 1}

Clerkenwell

Though calm in the day, creative Clerkenwell comes alive at night as office workers stream into its pubs, bars and restaurants. {map 1}

Covent Garden

Londoners might not live in this historic shopping district but they do pop by, weaving around tourists and street performers to pick up coffee and run their day's errands. {map 1}

Fulham

Largely home to the high-earning, Fulham is quiet during the week. But come the weekend, groups of friends pour into the area's cafés for brunch, families enjoy scenic riverside walks and football fans arrive for the beautiful game. {map 4}

Greenwich

When Londoners want to escape the city, they retreat to genteel Greenwich. Aside from its clutch of pubs and shops, Greenwich has grand naval buildings and a sprawling park – the perfect backdrop for picnics. {map 6}

Hackney

Forget Shoreditch; Hackney is the real hipster's paradise. Edgy and innovative, the area is awash with craft breweries, artisan bakeries and street art, not forgetting a glut of street food and vintage markets. {map 3}

Islington

Grand townhouses, chi-chi boutiques and top-quality restaurants have long attracted liberal elites to this part of the city. But it's not all champagne socialism. In Angel, the area's heart, down-to-earth comedy clubs and music venues keep the masses entertained. {map 2}

Kensington

Visitors flock to stately Kensington for the Natural History Museum, Science Museum and V&A. Affluent locals stay on for the posh dining spots and top-notch shopping. {map 4}

Notting Hill

Forget what you saw on the big screen: Notting Hill is as diverse as they come, with pastel-hued houses overlooked by tower blocks and its backstreets lined with assorted restaurants. This is also the home of the city's most joyous carnival. {map 4}

Nunhead

A stone's throw from trendy Peckham is sleepy Nunhead. The area flies under the radar despite its community-minded shops and lovely green spaces. {map 5}

Peckham

Sorry, Brixton, but it's all about Peckham these days. It's buzzy, multicultural and fast becoming a foodie destination. Creatives also love the area for its uber-cool arts spaces. {map 5}

Shoreditch

This was the heartland of alternative east London in the 90s, though it's done up to the nines these days. That said, Shoreditch remains a heartland for creatives and foodies. {map 2}

Soho

Sex shops hark back to Soho's history as London's red light district but today the area is better known for its LGBTQ+ nightlife and fab dining scene. {map 1}

South Bank

This cultural hub is a local icon. Londoners might not live here but they regularly attend performances at the Southbank Centre, or sip evening drinks beside the river and take in the view of the London Eye and Houses of Parliament. {map 5}

Spitalfields

Old meets new in Spitalfields and nearby Brick Lane, both areas of past immigration that now tempt Londoners to their fancy precincts, vintage markets and curry houses. {map 2}

Stoke Newington

Fast gentrifying but still genuinely multicultural, with a strong Jewish community, Stokey is loved for its indie shops, brunch spots and village feel. {map 3}

London
ON THE MAP

Whether you're looking for your new favourite spot or want to check out what each part of London has to offer, our maps – along with handy map references throughout the book – have you covered.

6

EDGWARE

COLINDALE

HENDON

HARROW

WEMBLEY

WILLESDEN

EALING

ACTON

HAYES

SOUTHALL

WEST DRAYTON

BRENTFORD

KEW

Kew Gardens

BARNES

HEATHROW

HOUNSLOW

RICHMOND

TWICKENHAM

Richmond Park

FELTHAM

HAM

Wimbledon Common

STAINES

ASHFORD

SUNBURY

Bushy Park

KINGSTON-UPON THAMES

River Thames

MOLESEY

CHERTSEY

WALTON-ON THAMES

ESHER

0 kilometres   4

0 miles   4

EWELL

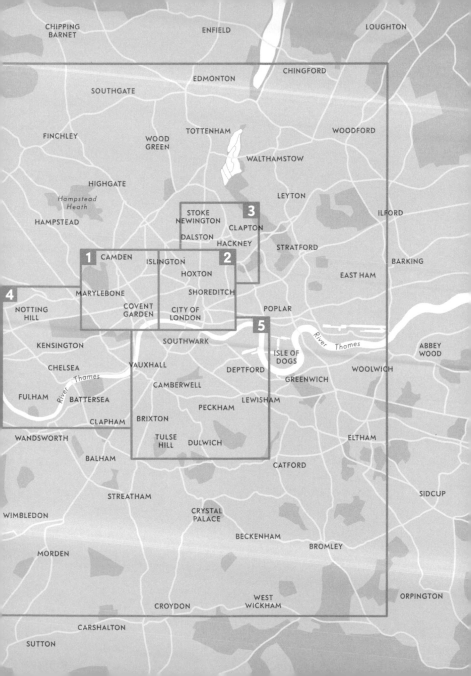

N Roundhouse

E Cheese Bar

S Camden Market

O Paddleboard on Regent's Canal

A Kentish Town Road

CAMDEN

N Jazz Cafe

A The Jewish Museum

BARNSBURY

D Spiritland

E The Coal Office

S Word on the Water

KING'S CROSS

D Big Chill House

The Story Garden **O**

The Crypt Gallery **A**

S Gay's The Word

Coram's Fields

The Postal Museum **A**

Regent's Park

S The Conran Shop

MARYLEBONE

S Daunt Books

Russell Square

BLOOMSBURY

Gray's Inn

N All Star Lanes

British Museum **A**

HOLBORN

E Rovi

Omotesando Koffee **D**

100 Club **N**

N Flight Club

Cavendish Square

Lincoln's Inn Fields

COVENT GARDEN

Workshop Coffee **D**

The Photographers' Gallery **A**

Freud **D**

OXFORD STREET

SOHO

Phonica **S**

Reckless Records **E**

Monmouth Coffee **D**

Seven Dials Market **E**

She Soho **N**

Stanfords **S**

Bao **E** **E** Mildreds

Choosing Keeping **S**

A London Transport Museum

180 The Strand **A**

Kiln **E**

COVENT GARDEN

The Crystal Maze LIVE Experience

LEICESTER SQUARE

MAYFAIR

PICCADILLY CIRCUS

D The Harp

0 metres 500

0 yards 500

National Gallery **A**

TRAFALGAR SQUARE

Waterloo Bridge

MAP 1

🄴 EAT

Bao *(p51)*
Caravan *(p34)*
Cheese Bar *(p48)*
The Coal Office *(p33)*
Exmouth Market *(p43)*
Kiln *(p36)*
Mildreds *(p44)*
Rovi *(p37)*
Sessions Arts Club *(p38)*
Seven Dials Market *(p42)*

🄳 DRINK

The Albion *(p66)*
Big Chill House *(p69)*
Freud *(p60)*
The Harp *(p73)*
Monmouth Coffee *(p57)*
Omotesando Koffee *(p59)*
Spiritland *(p62)*
Workshop Coffee *(p59)*
Ye Olde Cheshire Cheese *(p73)*

🅂 SHOP

Camden Market *(p103)*
Choosing Keeping *(p96)*
The Conran Shop *(p99)*
Daunt Books *(p92)*
Gay's the Word *(p93)*
Phonica *(p90)*
Reckless Records *(p90)*
Stanfords *(p93)*
Word on the Water *(p93)*

🄰 ARTS & CULTURE

180 The Strand *(p120)*
British Museum *(p119)*
The Crypt Gallery *(p120)*
The Jewish Museum *(p109)*
Kentish Town Road *(p114)*
London Transport Museum *(p108)*
National Gallery *(p117)*
The Photographers' Gallery *(p121)*
The Postal Museum *(p109)*

🄽 NIGHTLIFE

100 Club *(p143)*
All Star Lanes *(p138)*
The Crystal Maze LIVE Experience *(p137)*
Flight Club *(p136)*
Jazz Cafe *(p141)*
Roundhouse *(p140)*
Sadler's Wells *(p145)*
She Soho *(p153)*

🄾 OUTDOORS

Culpeper Community Garden *(p178)*
Paddleboard on Regent's Canal *(p168)*
The Story Garden *(p176)*

DALSTON

S Flashback Records

Regent's Canal

The Glory **N**

D 69 Colebrooke Row
N The Bill Murray

S Annie's

ISLINGTON

HAGGERSTON

Haggerston Park

Shoreditch Park

Hackney City Farm **O**

HACKNEY ROAD

Columbia Road **S**
The Royal Oak **D** Flower Market

HOXTON

Modern Calligraphy at **A**
Vintage Heaven

Bethnal Green **N**
Working Men's Club

FINSBURY

BETHNAL GREEN

Neon Naked Life Drawing

A Rivington Street

N Ballie Ballerson

OLD STREET

N XOYO

A
E Nobu

SHOREDITCH

N Boxpark

Bunhill Fields **O**
Burial Ground

Village Underground

A Brick Lane
Rough **S**
A Trade East

Brick Lane **S**
Vintage Market

D Queen of Hoxton

N Junkyard Golf Club

A
Dennis Severs' **S** Libreria
House

St John **S**
Bread & Wine

FARRINGDON

N Barbican
Centre

Old Spitalfields Market

SPITALFIELDS

S Smithfields
Meat Market

Eataly **N**

Gunpowder **E**
D Pangea Café

LONDON
WALL

BISHOPSGATE

COMMERCIAL STREET

Unity Diner **E**

CITY ROAD

HOLBORN

WHITECHAPEL

CHEAPSIDE

CITY OF
LONDON

CANNON ST

ALDGATE

LEMAN ST

Wilton's **N**
Music Hall

UPPER THAMES STREET

O Mudlarking on
the North Bank

A Black History Walk

Blackfriars
Bridge

Southwark
Bridge

London
Bridge

TOWER HILL

Thames

SOUTHWARK

0 metres   500
0 yards   500

ESSEX ROAD

UPPER STREET

NEW NORTH ROAD

CITY ROAD

KINGSLAND ROAD

GREAT EASTERN ST

MAP 2

HACKNEY

London Fields

2

Bistrotheque **E**

CAMBRIDGE HEATH

Phytology Medicinal Garden **O**

O
Satan's Whiskers

Renegade London Winery **D**

ROAD
E G Kelly

BETHNAL GREEN

WHITECHAPEL

ROAD

E Lahore Kebab House

SHADWELL

THE HIGHWAY
N Adonis at E1

WAPPING

E EAT

D DRINK

S SHOP

A ARTS & CULTURE

N NIGHTLIFE

O OUTDOORS

Abney Park Cemetery **O**

The Good Egg **E**

STOKE NEWINGTON

The White Hart **D**

NORTHWOLD ROAD

Millfields Park

STOKE NEWINGTON HIGH ST

UPPER CLAPTON ROAD

LEA BRIDGE ROAD

CLAPTON

Millfields Coffee **E**

STOKE NEWINGTON RD

LOWER CLAPTON ROAD

Hackney Downs

Beyond Retro **S**

SHACKLEWELL

EartH **N**

Black Cat Café **E**

Dalston Superstore **N**

Conservatory Archives **S**

The Karaoke Hole **N**

Ridley Road Market Bar **N**

DALSTON LANE

Hackney Church Brew Co. **D**

Paper Dress Vintage **S**

Dark Arts Coffee **D**

Dalston Roofpark **D**

Allpress Espresso Roastery & Cafe **D**

BALLS POND ROAD

Dalston Eastern Curve Garden **O**

GRAHAM ROAD

HACKNEY

DALSTON

Untitled **D**

Andu Café **E**

Pophams **D**

Kristina Records **S**

MARE STREET

London Fields Lido **O**

WELL STREET

The Haggerston **N**

KINGSLAND ROAD

Burley Fisher Books **S**

The Flower Appreciation Society **A**

O London Fields

Clay Work Sessions at Kana **A**

Candlemaking at Earl of East **A**

MARE STREET

Netil360 **N**

Mare Street Market **D**

Towpath Café **E**

Regent's Canal

Broadway Market **S**

VICTORIA PARK ROAD

CAMBRIDGE HEATH ROAD

Shoreditch Park

Haggerston Park

HAGGERSTON

CAMBRIDGE HEATH

Victoria Park Market **E**

0 metres 500
0 yards 500

HACKNEY ROAD

MAP 3

3

CLAPTON
PARK

HOMERTON

HOMERTON HIGH ST

The Spread
Eagle

CASSLAND ROAD

ROAD

People's Park **D**
Tavern

GROVE

Victoria
Park

ROAD

East London
Liquor Company
D

The Palm **D**
Tree

E EAT

Andu Café *(p44)*
Black Cat Café *(p46)*
The Good Egg *(p32)*
Millfields Coffee *(p34)*
The Spread Eagle *(p45)*
Towpath Café *(p34)*
Victoria Park Market *(42)*

D DRINK

Allpress Espresso Roastery
   & Cafe *(p59)*
Dalston Roofpark *(p69)*
Dark Arts Coffee *(p56)*
East London Liquor Company *(p78)*
Hackney Church Brew Co. *(p79)*
Netil360 *(p70)*
The Palm Tree *(p75)*
People's Park Tavern *(p67)*
Pophams *(p56)*
Untitled *(p63)*
The White Hart *(p65)*

S SHOP

Beyond Retro *(p86)*
Broadway Market *(p100)*
Burley Fisher Books *(p95)*
Conservatory Archives *(p99)*
Kristina Records *(p91)*
Paper Dress Vintage *(p86)*

A ARTS & CULTURE

Candlemaking at Earl of East *(p126)*
The Flower Appreciation
   Society *(p125)*
Clay Work Sessions at Kana *(p126)*

N NIGHTLIFE

Dalston Superstore *(p151)*
EartH *(p142)*
The Haggerston *(p140)*
The Karaoke Hole *(p155)*
Mare Street Market *(p134)*
Ridley Road Market Bar *(p151)*

O OUTDOORS

Abney Park Cemetery *(p172)*
Dalston Eastern Curve
   Garden *(p178)*
London Fields *(p166)*
London Fields Lido *(p160)*
Victoria Park *(p165)*

Regent's Park

MAIDA VALE

Kensal Green Cemetery ⊙

NORTH KENSINGTON

Grand Union Canal

WESTWAY

Alfies Antiques Market **S**

EDGWARE

MARYLEBONE ROAD

MARYLEBONE

Waterbus Rides to Camden ⊙

PADDINGTON

OXFORD

LADBROKE GROVE

Portobello Road Market **S**

Portobello Wall Public Art Project **A**

BAYSWATER

BAYSWATER ROAD

Hyde Park

PARK LANE

MAYFAIR

NOTTING HILL

Music and Video Exchange **S**

Kensington Gardens

Serpentine Lido ⊙

PICCADILLY

Green Park

HOLLAND PARK AVENUE

Royal Trinity Hospice **S**

Holland Park

KENSINGTON ROAD

KNIGHTSBRIDGE

KENSINGTON HIGH STREET

KENSINGTON

Science Museum **A**

Natural History Museum **A**

A V&A

SLOANE ST

CROMWELL ROAD

SOUTH KENSINGTON

WEST KENSINGTON

Saatchi Gallery **A**

CHELSEA

FULHAM ROAD

KING'S ROAD

Ranelagh Gardens

LILLIE ROAD

Brompton Cemetery ⊙

Market Hall Fulham **E**

CHELSEA EMBANKMENT

Thames

Battersea Park

FULHAM PALACE ROAD

FULHAM

NEW KING'S ROAD

BATTERSEA BRIDGE RD

The Magic Garden **D**

BATTERSEA PARK RD

E Mien Tay

Sightsee aboard the Thames Clipper ⊙

Walk the Thames Path ⊙

YORK ROAD

BATTERSEA

PUTNEY

The Ship **D**

0 kilometres ⎯⎯⎯⎯ 1

0 miles ⎯⎯⎯⎯ 1

MAP 4

4

BLOOMSBURY

STREET

SOHO CHARING CROSS RD

St James's Park

WESTMINSTER

VAUXHALL BRIDGE RD

Tate Britain Ⓐ

PIMLICO

GROSVENOR RD

NINE ELMS LANE

NINE ELMS

Ⓔ EAT

Market Hall Fulham *(p43)*
Mien Tay *(p37)*

Ⓓ DRINK

The Magic Garden *(p65)*
The Ship *(p64)*

Ⓢ SHOP

Alfies Antiques Market *(p84)*
Music and Video Exchange *(p91)*
Portobello Road Market *(p85)*
Royal Trinity Hospice *(p85)*

Ⓐ ARTS & CULTURE

Natural History Museum *(p116)*
Portobello Wall Public Art Project *(113)*
Saatchi Gallery *(p122)*
Science Museum *(p119)*
Tate Britain *(p119)*
V&A *(p117)*

Ⓞ OUTDOORS

Brompton Cemetery *(p175)*
Kensal Green Cemetery *(p173)*
Serpentine Lido *(p160)*
Sightsee aboard the Thames Clipper *(p168)*
Walk the Thames Path *(p169)*
Waterbus Rides to Camden *(p171)*

Queen
Elizabeth
Hall Roof
Garden **S**
D Lyaness at Sea
Containers
Blackfriars
Bridge
A Tate Modern
London
Bridge
WAPPING
Southbank **S** South Bank
Centre **D** Book Market
A Hawksmoor **E**
E Padella
Tower
Bridge
SOUTH **E** Southbank Centre
Food Market
Flat Iron Square **N**
Omeara **N**
E Electric Shuffle
BANK
Hutong
Thames
Westminster
Bridge
The Old Vic **N**
SOUTHWARK
Maltby Street
Market
A Leake Street Tunnel
White Cube **A**
E D Hawkes Cidery and Tap Room
A
Thames
N Mercato
Metropolitano
D
JAMAICA RD
The National Covid
Memorial Wall
Bermondsey
Distillery
Southwark
Park
LAMBETH ROAD
ELEPHANT
AND CASTLE
E Spa Terminus
BERMONDSEY
OLD KENT ROAD
D Tamesis Dock
WALWORTH ROAD
Above the Stag
Theatre
N
N Vauxhall City Farm
N Royal Vauxhall Tavern
Burgess
Park
OLD KENT ROAD
VAUXHALL
Kennington
Park
CAMBERWELL NEW ROAD
CAMBERWELL
CLAPHAM ROAD
PECKHAM ROAD
QUEEN'S ROAD
BRIXTON ROAD
Lumberjack **D**
Persepolis **E**
PECKHAM
STOCKWELL
N Brixton Jamm
Peckham Audio **N**
N Frank's
A Pottery at The Kiln Rooms
N Kanpai
COLDHARBOUR LANE
DENMARK HILL
Ruskin
Park
Four Quarters **N**
Nunhead
Gardener **S**
Brixton Village and
Market Row
BRIXTON
Nunhead
Cemetery **O**
D
Duke of
Edinburgh
S Pop Brixton
N
D S D S Rachel and Malika's
A Brixton Street Art
EAST
DULWICH
NUNHEAD
ACRE LANE
Prince of
Wales
Three
Eight Four
PECKHAM RYE
S Forest
The Ivy House **D**
N Gremio de Brixton
LORDSHIP LANE
Rye Books **N**
Peckham Rye
Park
Hootananny **N**
HERNE
HILL
HERNE HILL
Brockwell Lido **O**
E Peachy Goat
O Brockwell
Park
DULWICH
TULSE HILL
D Bullfinch Brewery
0 kilometres   1
0 miles   1
Bel Air
Park
Dulwich
Park

MAP 5

5

◉ Surrey Docks Farm

ROTHERHITHE

EVELYN STREET

Ⓝ Big Dyke Energy

NEW CROSS

Ⓐ London Terrariums

BROCKLEY

Brockley's Rock Ⓔ

Brockley ◉ Cemetery

Camberwell Cemetery

Ⓔ EAT

Brockley's Rock *(p51)*
Hawksmoor *(p37)*
Hutong *(p38)*
Maltby Street Market *(p40)*
Padella *(p48)*
Peachy Goat *(p45)*
Persepolis *(p46)*
Southbank Centre Food Market *(p41)*
Spa Terminus *(p42)*

Ⓓ DRINK

Bermondsey Distillery *(p78)*
Bullfinch Brewery *(p76)*
Duke of Edinburgh *(p64)*
Frank's *(p68)*
Hawkes Cidery and Tap Room *(p77)*
The Ivy House *(p75)*
Kanpai *(p76)*
Lyaness at Sea Containers *(p60)*
Lumberjack (p57)
Prince of Wales *(p71)*
Queen Elizabeth Hall Roof Garden *(p70)*
Tamesis Dock *(p70)*
Three Eight Four *(p62)*

Ⓢ SHOP

Brixton Village and Market Row *(p103)*
Forest *(p96)*
Nunhead Gardener *(p97)*
Rachel and Malika's *(p98)*
Rye Books *(p92)*
South Bank Book Market *(p103)*

Ⓐ ARTS & CULTURE

Brixton Street Art *(p114)*
Leake Street Tunnel *(p112)*
London Terrariums *(p126)*
The National Covid Memorial Wall *(p111)*
Pottery at The Kiln Rooms *(p124)*
Tate Modern *(p116)*
White Cube *(p121)*

Ⓝ NIGHTLIFE

Above the Stag Theatre *(p153)*
Big Dyke Energy *(p155)*
Brixton Jamm *(p150)*
Electric Shuffle *(p136)*
Flat Iron Square *(p133)*
Four Quarters *(p138)*
Gremio de Brixton *(p149)*
Hootananny *(p142)*
Mercato Metropolitano *(p134)*
The Old Vic *(p147)*
Omeara *(p142)*
Peckham Audio *(p148)*
Pop Brixton *(p135)*
Royal Vauxhall Tavern *(p152)*
Southbank Centre *(p147)*

Ⓞ OUTDOORS

Brockley Cemetery *(p175)*
Brockwell Lido *(p161)*
Brockwell Park *(p166)*
Nunhead Cemetery *(p174)*
Surrey Docks Farm *(p177)*
Vauxhall City Farm *(p177)*

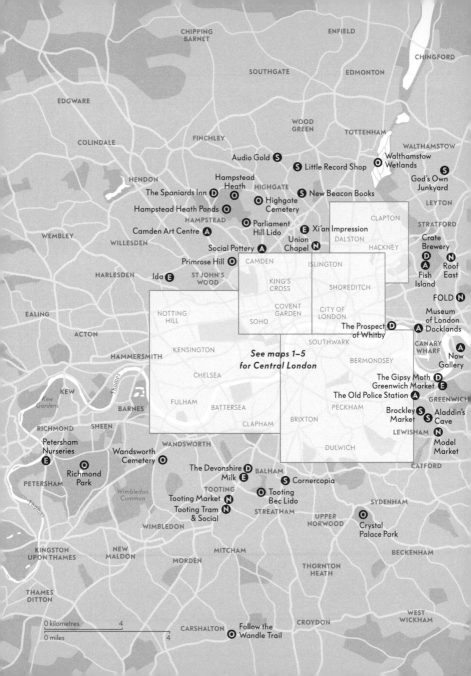

MAP 6

🅔 EAT

Greenwich Market *(p40)*
Ida *(p38)*
Milk *(p35)*
Petersham Nurseries *(p39)*
Xi'an Impression *(p49)*

🅓 DRINK

Crate Brewery *(p78)*
The Devonshire *(p75)*
The Gipsy Moth *(p67)*
The Prospect of Whitby *(p66)*
The Spaniards Inn *(p72)*

🆂 SHOP

Aladdin's Cave *(p84)*
Audio Gold *(p88)*
Brockley Market *(p101)*
Cornercopia *(p98)*
God's Own Junkyard *(p98)*
Little Record Shop *(p88)*
New Beacon Books *(p95)*

🅐 ARTS & CULTURE

Camden Art Centre *(p123)*
East End Women's Museum *(p111)*
Fish Island *(p114)*
Museum of London
 Docklands *(p108)*

Now Gallery *(p123)*
The Old Police Station *(p122)*
Social Pottery *(p125)*

🅝 NIGHTLIFE

FOLD *(p149)*
Model Market *(p133)*
Roof East *(p139)*
Tooting Market *(p135)*
Tooting Tram & Social *(p150)*
Union Chapel *(p141)*

🅞 OUTDOORS

Charlton Lido *(p161)*
Crystal Palace Park *(p167)*
Follow the Wandle Trail *(p169)*
Hampstead Heath *(p165)*
Hampstead Heath Ponds *(p162)*
Highgate Cemetery *(p172)*
Parliament Hill Lido *(p162)*
Primrose Hill *(p166)*
Richmond Park *(p164)*
Tooting Bec Lido *(p162)*
Walthamstow Wetlands *(p171)*
Wandsworth Cemetery *(p174)*

EAT

Food comes in many guises in London: unhurried brunches, cosy pub roasts, sociable street food feasts. Whatever the meal, it's all about good food and good company.

Brunch Spots

Whether it's a jubilant affair with pals or a lingering feast for two, brunch is the hallmark of a proper weekend. And London is chock-full of brunch spots to lure locals away from the comfort of bed.

THE GOOD EGG

Map 3; 93 Stoke Newington Church Street, Stoke Newington; ///friend.fuels.pram; www.thegoodegg.co

The Good Egg's all-day breakfasts have become a queue-inducing weekend ritual for Stokey's effortlessly trendy locals. The café's calm nook of wooden tables, stripped floorboards and whitewashed walls lined with jars of pickled lemons forms a backdrop for the exchanging of stories: families pass around sweet braided babka,

Try it!
MAKE A BAGEL

Fancy brunch at home? Order an At-Home Bagel Kit from The Good Egg. It comes with pastrami-spiced smoked salmon, finish-at-home sesame bagels, schmear and a bottle of cava.

friends gather over Jerusalem-inspired sharing plates and the slightly dishevelled toast to the hair of the dog with the joyful clink of Prosecco glasses.

ST JOHN BREAD & WINE

Map 2; 94–6 Commercial Street, Shoreditch; ///exit.cover.rods; www.stjohnrestaurant.com

Nothing says confidence like a short, simple menu. And St John's stripped-back breakfast, offering a handful of old-school classics like bacon sandwiches and grilled kippers on sourdough, is rightly confident. Maybe it's the rare-breed bacon, or the nose-to-tail philosophy – whatever it is, St John's has become a local institution and a great place to fuel up before browsing Spitalfields Market.

» Don't leave without bagging your own fresh made-to-order madeleines – the perfect sweet finish to a savoury brunch.

THE COAL OFFICE

Map 1; 2 Bagley Walk, Coal Drops Yard, Kings Cross; ///rooms.inch.shaky https://coaloffice.com

In-the-know Londoners were there the minute Coal Drops Yard opened, snapping away at this industrial sweep of Victorian railway arches transformed with concept stores and stylish restaurants. And they were there when The Coal Office – a meeting of minds between designer Tom Dixon and chef Assaf Granit – launched. Those first fans still haven't left; join them on the terrace for coffees and sharing plates of Middle Eastern-inspired dishes.

MILLFIELDS COFFEE
Map 3; 145 Chatsworth Road, Clapton; ///delay.safety.cove;
www.millfieldscoffee.co.uk

Under pastel-pink signage and with an airy dining room that spills onto a generous slab of pavement opposite Millfields Park, this is a favourite spot for young couples with gurgling babies and catch-ups with friends over brews. It's a slice of low-key Clapton life, especially on Sundays thanks to the proper East End market just outside.

TOWPATH CAFÉ
Map 3; 42 De Beauvoir Crescent, Haggerston; ///erase.gears.face;
www.towpathlondon.com

The trio of food-fanatics that run this canalside caff have garnered a cult following for their cheese toasties, but hipsters keep coming back for the coffee, changing menu and cheerful, casual set-up. Settle in on the makeshift furniture and let your entertainment be the constant stream of bikes whizzing along the canal.

» Don't leave without swinging by Batch Baby, just down the road, for a post-brunch latte and pet of Porridge the dog.

CARAVAN
Map 1; 11–13 Exmouth Market, Farringdon; ///strike.decide.sings;
www.caravanrestaurants.co.uk

Billed as "well-travelled food" owing to its globally inspired sharing plates, this small London chain dishes up mouthwatering fusion fare: think a whole burrata with bergamot, fennel and coriander seeds.

If Caravan is full, nab a spot at nearby Berber & Q, where you'll find small plates and Middle Eastern spices.

Pair with a flat white from the in-house roastery and you'll be set up for exploring Exmouth Market. Grab a table on its corner-side terrace if you can.

MILK

Map 6; 18–20 Bedford Hill, Balham; ///melt.give.trucks;
www.milklondonshop.uk

This spot at the tail end of Balham's Hildreth Market is no secret. It's a place to see and be seen, where queuing for an hour on a Saturday is a rite of passage. Milk may not be as fairly priced as some of the smaller spots that line the same street, but the setting is unbeatable. Join fashionable groups sipping on coffees alfresco – come rain or shine – and watch flower traders sell their blooms at the other end of the cobblestone street.

BISTROTHEQUE

Map 2; 23–27 Wadeson Street, Bethnal Green;
///regard.open.amuse; www.bistrotheque.com

Don't be fooled by the industrial exterior of Bistrotheque. Enveloped in an interior of greys and whites, this is where Londoners head when they want to show how grown up they are. Parents in town? In-laws visiting? A birthday brunch without the all-you-can-drink connotations? The above would all work nicely here, especially if the pianist makes an appearance. And the food – modern fusion dishes that meld unusual ingredients and British produce – is set to impress too.

Special Occasion

*Birthday celebrations, a well-earned promotion,
the keys to a new home: whatever you're raising a
toast to, London has a truly memorable dining
experience ready and waiting.*

KILN

Map 1; 58 Brewer Street, Soho; ///stray.puppy.gains; www.kilnsoho.com

The style at this Thai barbecue restaurant is performative – a counter runs the length of the compact space giving diners a view of the open-kitchen – but the atmosphere is casual. Inspired by Thai roadside eateries, the food here comprises flame-licked meats and ember-charred vegetables. Repeat customers head to the back to talk to the chefs over the soundtrack of chatter and bubbling pots.

NOBU

**Map 2; 10–50 Willow Street, Shoreditch; ///arts.hired.asset;
www.noburestaurants.com**

Sleek concrete, seductive lighting and a back-lit bar – if you needed proof that once-gritty Shoreditch has grown up then this is it. Set in the Nobu hotel, this spot draws a stylish clientele who pore over delicate Japanese-Peruvian dishes (think slivers of sashimi and piles of ceviche).

MIEN TAY

Map 4; 122 Kingsland Road, Hackney; ///option.care.poet;
www. mientay.co.uk

This homely southwest Vietnamese kitchen is a legend of "pho mile" – the stretch of Vietnamese restaurants between Shoreditch and Hoxton. Come a birthday, loyal groups of Hackney locals pile in, clutching bottles of wine (it's BYO) and ordering plates of butter-soft galangal goat curry to pass around their jovial party.

HAWKSMOOR

Map 5; 16 Winchester Walk, Borough; ///spot.oiled.ties;
www.thehawksmoor.com

With eight branches across London, Hawksmoor could get a bit too big for its boots, but it keeps ticking all the boxes with its sustainably sourced steak. The Borough branch is always packed on Sundays with sophisticated patrons splashing out on wallet-draining roasts.

ROVI

Map 1; 59 Wells Street, Fitzrovia; ///points.closer.purely;
www.ottolenghi.co.uk

Israeli-English chef Yotam Ottolenghi is a local icon famed for his inventive creations, and his Fitzrovia restaurant promises a special meal without the waiting list. Cleverly executed vegetable dishes take the lead here, while meat and fish play supporting roles.

» Don't leave without tucking into the celeriac shawarma, especially if you're a meat-eater – you'll forget this kebab is veggie.

HUTONG

**Map 5; Level 33, The Shard, 31 St Thomas Street, London Bridge;
///villa.epic.pound; www.hutong.co.uk**

Any special occasion is made extra memorable by a spectacular
view. The Shard has a number of swanky restaurants but Hutong's
panoramic views, northern Chinese menu and creative cocktail list
take some beating. There's also a fixed-price lunch menu, making
for both an affordable and stellar meal.

IDA

**Map 6; 167 Fifth Avenue, Queen's Park; ///liability.wooden.bump;
www.idarestaurant.co.uk**

Named after chef Avi's mother, this old-school trattoria oozes
old-world Italian charm with its wood panelling, starched tablecloths
and vintage artworks. Avi and his wife Simonetta will make you and
your party feel like long-lost family, insisting you try the hand-rolled
pappardelle and topping up your glasses of Chianti. And why
shouldn't you have another? You're celebrating, after all.

SESSIONS ARTS CLUB

**Map 1; Old Sessions House, 24 Clerkenwell Green, Clerkenwell; ///rise.
prone.aspect; www.sessionsartsclub.com**

Anniversary around the corner? Book a table at this gorgeous dining
club, tucked away in an old courthouse. Push through the red front
door, where a receptionist will check your reservation and point you
in the direction of the rickety lift. After a short ride you'll arrive in what

was once the judge's dining room, today replete with modern artworks lit by candlelight on the peeling walls. Clink glasses with your beloved while smiley staff deliver you sharing plates like panisse (addictive chickpea chips) and succulent squid, tomato and calamarata.

>> Don't leave without visiting the plush bathroom for hidden views of Old Sessions House and curious stained-glass toilet doors.

GUNPOWDER

Map 2; 11 White's Row, Spitalfields; ///email.sheets.adding; www.gunpowderlondon.com

A mother-and-son team runs this tiny Indian restaurant in Spitalfields, where big occasions are celebrated with big sharing menus. The sophisticated small plates include Kashmiri lamb chops and a whole broccoli head doused in yoghurt and spices. Wash it all down with a round of chilli-spiked mimosas, which gets spicier as you drink.

PETERSHAM NURSERIES

Map 6; Off Church Lane, Petersham Road, Richmond; ///smile.voices.liked; www.petershamnurseries.com

You'd struggle to find a more beautiful setting; tucked down a muddy lane, this oasis feels nothing like London. Set within a garden centre, the glasshouse restaurant transports you to the Med: a bougainvillea-draped ceiling, bowls full of lemons atop worn wooden tables and the heady scent of jasmine. It's as much about the setting as it is the menu, which is inspired by the nursery garden and what's in season. After lunch, treat yourself to something in the shop – you deserve it.

Street Food

On a budget? Some of the best food in London is dished up from food trucks and makeshift stalls. Try everything: you might be sampling the work of the city's next big chef.

GREENWICH MARKET

**Map 6; 5B Greenwich Market, Greenwich; ///darker.forum.doors;
www.greenwichmarket.london**

They say half the fun is getting there – arrive in Greenwich by boat and you've certainly started things off right. Follow your nose, and the locals, to its historical covered market, held daily. Surrounded by independents, the street food stalls offer a wealth of options: the fragrantly spiced pomegranate-speckled wraps, gooey brownies and flaky empanadas all have a loyal following.

MALTBY STREET MARKET

Map 5; Ropewalk, Bermondsey; ///grabs.fled.actors; www.maltby.st

Forget the hubbub of Borough Market. Come the weekend and London's foodies have one place in mind – Maltby Street Market. Bermondsey's Ropewalk, a narrow passage between Victorian railway arches strung with festoon lights and fluttering flags, makes

Maltby Street Market is the perfect place to fuel up before tackling Bermondsey's beloved Beer Mile.

an attractive backdrop. Run the gourmet gauntlet between traders, or duck into the railway arches to discover *jamón* shops and small-batch gin bars.

SOUTHBANK CENTRE FOOD MARKET

Map 5; Belvedere Road, South Bank; ///rift.stews.dips;
www.southbankcentre.co.uk

A trip to the South Bank is an absolute must for any visitor to London – it's hard to beat the cultural centre's city vistas and the lively atmosphere along the riverside walkway. Time your arrival for a late lunch at this small but perfectly formed weekend food market, tucked just behind the Royal Festival Hall. Some of London's most delicious dishes can be sampled here, and there's always time for a freshly poured ale, best enjoyed on a Thameside bench looking onto the Houses of Parliament and the London Eye.

» Don't leave without trying one of The Frenchie's famous duck confit burgers with melted cheese and duck fat-fried chips.

Try it!
JOIN A BAKING CLASS

Near Maltby Street you'll find busy Borough Market and baking school Bread Ahead *(www.breadahead.com)*. Join a half-day course and learn how to make buttery croissants or oil-rich focaccia bread.

SPA TERMINUS

Map 5; Dockley Road Industrial Estate, Bermondsey;
///spins.wooden.minute; www.spa-terminus.co.uk

Spa Terminus is the place locals really don't want to share. Here
the railway arches are home to the headquarters of some of the
city's best independent food businesses, which on Saturdays open
to the public. Join sets of 30-something friends as they peruse the
organic vegetables, biodynamic wines and artisan cheeses – all
while clutching invigorating cups of Monmouth coffee.

VICTORIA PARK MARKET

Map 3; Entrance via Bonner Gate, Victoria Park, Bow;
///occupy.cases.noise; www.victoriaparkmarket.com

East London's biggest open space is the ideal setting for a Sunday
parade of artisan food and drink stands. Here, trendy East Enders
supplement their weekly shop with meat from organic butchers,
small-batch baked goods, farm-made pies and vegan cheese.
There's even a dog deli, where locals spoil their pooches silly with
deer trotters and salmon jerky before a run around the park.

SEVEN DIALS MARKET

Map 1; 35 Earlham Street, Covent Garden; ///mess.army.flip;
www.sevendialsmarket.com

This centrally located spot is often overlooked by visitors, but
Londoners love this indoor food hall, which is open Friday through
Monday. Here you'll discover a tempting variety of food outlets

at street level, serving a diverse selection of food and cocktails. Head downstairs to eat at communal tables with professionals breaking for lunch or gaggles of friends welcoming the weekend with rounds of beers.

EXMOUTH MARKET

Map 1; Exmouth Market, Clerkenwell; ///prep.empty.teach; www.exmouth.london

Come lunchtime, make a beeline for this pedestrianized street of food stalls, open every Monday through Saturday. There are just a dozen stands, so be sure you get there sooner rather than later – it's so popular that local workers will have snapped up most of the food by 2pm. Hang around the area until the evening, when it's time for after-work beers and table football at Café Kick.

» Don't leave without trying a steaming bowl of Ghanaian lamb stew, fried plantain and tomato-rich jollof rice from Spinach & Agushi.

MARKET HALL FULHAM

Map 4; 472 Fulham Road, Fulham; ///posed.rated.really; www.markethalls.co.uk

Tube stations and great food rarely go hand in hand but Fulham's Market Hall bucks this trend. Housed in an ornate Edwardian entrance hall that once served the Tube, this buzzing food market has become a local foodie favourite. Pencil pushers nip here for lunchtime kebabs, freelancers sip flat whites and tap away at laptops, and crowds arrive at night for plump fried chicken and drinks on the roof.

Plant-Based

Traditional British food may be meat-heavy but, here in the capital, veg-lovers won't go hungry; London's plant-based revolution is surviving and thriving. Here's just a flavour of the city's meat-free offerings.

MILDREDS

Map 1; 45 Lexington Street, Soho; ///marble.farm.member; www.mildreds.co.uk

With six locations scattered across the city, Mildreds is a vegan institution. We particularly love its original Soho outpost, which is split over several levels of a higgledy-piggledy townhouse. This is the place to while away a balmy summer evening, when the sash windows are thrown open, and tuck into Sri Lankan curry or quinoa kofte with tahini cream and freekeh.

ANDU CAFÉ

Map 3; 528 Kingsland Road, Dalston; ///risen.clip.pouch; www.anduvegancafe.com

Ethiopian cuisine might just be the world's most vegan-friendly, with spicy beans, pulses and greens in oil-rich curries. This cash-only canteen has been serving it up since 1970 – long before the vegan

While you're east, look out for Vegan Nights, when newbie DJs and vegan food trucks take over Truman Brewery.

trend hit Dalston. It's BYO, only charges £7 a head (takeaway spreads for a fiver) and feels like you're eating in a neighbour's living room.

THE SPREAD EAGLE

Map 3; 224 Homerton High Street, Hackney; ///glee.bonus.locate; www.thespreadeaglelondon.co.uk

London's first 100 per cent vegan pub was savvy enough to throw open its cruelty-free doors in Veganuary 2018, creating serious hype over its animal product-free beers. Today the coquettishly named Spread Eagle prides itself on its minimal-waste kitchen and pub grub made from locally produced and foraged ingredients. Come on a Sunday for the vegan roast; options include Beet Wellington and a crowd-pleasing walnut and cashew nut roast.

» Don't leave without trying the ploughman's lunch, complete with a porkless pie. It's great medicine on a drizzly day.

PEACHY GOAT

Map 5; 16 Half Moon Lane, Herne Hill; ///spend.wished.gross; www.peachygoat.com

Vegan versions of all the bistro classics you can imagine come together at this adorable café run by three childhood friends. The eco-conscious menu uses 100 per cent natural ingredients to make a range of hearty plates – from a mouthwatering "sausage" sandwich to a filling "blue cheese" burger to a decadent sticky toffee pudding.

UNITY DINER

Map 2; 60 Wentworth Street, Spitalfields; ///bonus.wiring.myself;
www.unitydiner.co.uk

Designed for vegans and flexitarians, this 100-seat, non-profit diner –
run by vegan activist Earthling Ed – is as much a centre for public
education around mass food production and animal cruelty as it is
a place to chow down on a soy Chikken burger with melted Cheeze.

BLACK CAT CAFÉ

Map 3; 76A Clarence Road, Hackney; ///intervals.cotton.rabble;
www.blackcatcafe.co.uk

You know you're onto a local secret when a restaurant with plain décor
and a few wooden benches is packed to the rafters. As well as epic
brunches, this independent workers' cooperative sells locally made
products and has a bookshop stocked with plant-based cookbooks.

» Don't leave without trying a homemade vegan sausage roll, which
varies in shape and size according to the batch of the day.

PERSEPOLIS

Map 5; 28–30 Peckham High Street, Peckham;
///decreased.match.wonderfully; www.foratasteofpersia.co.uk

This tiny little spot is wholly unapologetic about the fact that it's
essentially a handful of tables crammed between the shelves of a
corner shop. And likewise you won't be sorry when you try the café's
small plates of Middle Eastern vegan fare, best tackled with a gang
of pals. (There's a set fee per head and it's BYO.)

Liked by the locals

"What's unique about London is its huge variety, accessibility and density of vegan restaurants. You can get vegan fried chicken, cheesy stuffed crust pizza, healthy vegan food if you want to – and it's all happened in the past five years. It makes me excited to think where we'll be five years from now."

ED WINTER, UNITY DINER FOUNDER

Comfort Food

This is a city that loves to indulge, whether that's with silky noodles wrapped in butter, oozing cheese toasties or burgers sandwiched between glazed brioche buns. Now's not the time to hold back.

CHEESE BAR

Map 1; Unit 93–4 Camden Stables, Camden Town; ///rival.rivers.just; www.thecheesebar.com

The Cheese Bar has elevated melted cheese – that wonderful gooey pick-me-up – to higher ranks with this little nook of a restaurant decked out in industrial chic. Cheese fiends, get your fix here. Gobble handfuls of mozzarella sticks on the sun-dappled terrace or a bubbling pan of mac 'n' cheese at the bar.

PADELLA

Map 5; 6 Southwark Street, London Bridge; ///best.storm.little; www.padella.co

Pillowy ravioli, silken pappardelle, nostalgic nests of spaghetti – few comfort foods beat the carby embrace of pasta. And Padella brings an added layer of comfort to the dish, that of predictability: you can tell the time with one glance at this place. Mornings are a lull of calm, the

Cheat Padella's queue with WalkUp. As long as you're near, the app will queue for you, so you can enjoy a drink.

windows framing the ritual of rolling pasta; come noon a throng of office workers signals lunch; by evening the queue reappears, and inside hums with chatter.

G KELLY

Map 2; 526 Roman Road, Bow; ///newly.comb.tells; www.gkelly.london

Long wanted to taste the classic East End dish, jellied eels? Of course you have. And at G Kelly – where they've been rustling up that dish since 1939 – you're in safe hands. This is one of East London's last-remaining traditional pie and mash shops, a family business that closed only for a two-year refurb in 2017. Minced beef pie, with mash, parsley sauce "liquor" and eels, is especially popular with Cockney locals. There's even a vegan pie on the menu now, too.

XI'AN IMPRESSION

Map 6; 117 Benwell Road, Arsenal; ///summer.glove.punk;
www.xianimpression.co.uk

This tiny, BYO, strip-lit canteen almost didn't make it into this book – it's a neighbourhood secret that's too good to share. But we've decided to let you in on it. Chef Wei Guirong serves street food from the Shan Xi province of China, home to the Terracotta Warriors. And, oh boy, is she talented. The menu is all hand-pulled noodles, pot sticker dumplings and wonderfully gloopy pulled-pork "burgers". Comforting, bold-flavoured and dripping in juices, the food at Xi'an Impression might just change your life. But be a pal and keep it to yourself, eh?

Solo, Pair, Crowd

Whether you're grabbing a bite to eat on your own or feasting en masse, there's a foodie spot for you.

FLYING SOLO

Breakfast of champions

You won't find anywhere like E. Pellicci in Bethnal Green. The Italian greasy spoon's stellar fry-ups and strong builder's tea is favoured by East Enders who have lived in the area for decades. Drop in for a hearty breakkie and lively chat with the locals.

IN A PAIR

Pasta, glorious pasta

To fully appreciate Bancone's handmade pasta, select one lucky loved one who is as keen on reasonably priced, perfectly al dente Italian fare as you — and go all out.

FOR A CROWD

Competitive Sunday roasts

The Alma Pub in Newington Green is known for three things: first-rate roasts (you'll need to book ahead), its Sunday evening pub quizzes and the quirky movie memorabilia that dots its interior.

BAO

Map 1; 53 Lexington Street, Soho; ///decks.drift.clown; www.baolondon.com

Everything about this place is little (apart from the rather infamous queue to get in, that is): the tiny, pared-back interior; the short paper menu you scribble your selections on; the bite-sized steamed milk buns that have given their namesake restaurant this cult following. Diminutive yes, but this isn't dainty dining – expect to leave over-stuffed on bites of tender pork-confit bao and crispy fried chicken.

BROCKLEY'S ROCK

**Map 5; 317 Brockley Road, Brockley; ///cigar.meals.music;
www.brockleysrock.co.uk**

Few dishes beat fish and chips for pure comfort and – lucky for south Londoners – Brockley's Rock has won awards for its treatment of the British classic. Here, freshly cooked fish in a lip-smacking batter sits alongside hand-cut chips, with options for coeliacs and vegans, too.
» Don't leave without taking your fish and chips to nearby Hilly Fields park to tuck in with killer views of Lewisham and Canary Wharf.

LAHORE KEBAB HOUSE

**Map 2; 2–10 Umberston Street, Whitechapel; ///social.beats.outfit;
www.lahore-kebabhouse.com**

London wouldn't be London without its curry houses, and Pakistani-owned Lahore promises a truly comforting slap-up meal. Don't be fooled by this local icon's modest appearance; you'll find queues of hopefuls, all clutching bags of booze (it's BYO), here on weekends.

Feed your sweet tooth at
AMBALA

Queues snake out the door of
this Pakistani sweet shop during
religious festivals. Treat yourself
to *habshi halwa*, a fudgy
cardamom-infused cake made of
cashews, pistachios and almonds.

Stock up at
BHAVINS FOOD

Begin at one of Tooting's oldest
grocery stores and stock up on
spices to add to your collection.

LETCHWORTH STREET

BROADWATER

ROAD

1

2

3

UPPER TOOTING ROAD

Lunch at
MIRCH MASALA

Tuck into succulent slow-cooked
lamb at this Indian-Pakistani
institution, which is a favourite
of local politician Sadiq Khan.

Just off the main road –
which locals call "land
of the curry mile" – is
Harrington's, *which has*
been serving pie and
mash since 1908.

SELKIRK ROAD

BLAKENHAM ROAD

STREET

4

Raise a glass at
TOOTING MARKET

Walk off your lunch by browsing
Tooting Market, which has been
keeping residents' fridges stocked
since 1930. Fresh produce aside –
and if you still have room – there
are lots of street food options here.

TOOTING HIGH

TOTTERDOWN STREET

TOOTING
BROADWAY

0 metres   100
0 yards   100

An afternoon
dining in Tooting

Travel south and you'll find one of London's most vibrant neighbourhoods. Trendy new restaurants are constantly popping up around Tooting Broadway, adding to a buzzing food culture that's embedded in community spirit. Tooting High Street, which stretches between Tube stops Tooting Bec and Tooting Broadway, bustles with independent, Indian and Pakistani shops that reflect the multicultural demographics of the area. Come Eid or Diwali, there's no more exciting place to be, sampling locally made sweets and revelling in the celebratory atmosphere.

1. Bhavins Food
193–7 Upper
Tooting Road;
///sums.supporter.search

2. Ambala
201 Upper Tooting Road;
www.ambalafoods.com;
///soda.rope.sooner

3. Mirch Masala
213 Upper Tooting Road;
www.mirchmasala-

takeaway.co.uk
///tried.view.richer

4. Tooting Market
21–23 Tooting High Street;
www.tootingmarket.com
///shells.labs.straw

 Harrington's ///flood.
angle.scope

DRINK

Pubs and cafés are the beating heart of London's social scene. Days pass catching up in cute indie coffee shops, and nights are spent bantering in buzzing beer gardens.

Coffee Shops

London's coffee scene is thriving, with independent cafés mushrooming across the city, from artisan coffee shops showcasing their locally roasted brews to coffee bars plonked in the most unexpected places.

DARK ARTS COFFEE

Map 3; 1–5 Rosina Street, Homerton; ///serve.empire.frost; www.darkartscoffee.co.uk

Tattoos, beards, a sign declaring "I will kill again" – if you thought the dark arts were just found in *Harry Potter*, think again. This place has a rebellious streak: heavy metal plays, horror film ads line the walls and the owners will happily tell you they've never made a business decision sober. Take it in while sipping your coffee in the roastery.

POPHAMS

Map 3; 197 Richmond Road, Hackney; ///gosh.prices.slips; www.pophamsbakery.com

If you like your coffee with a little something to nibble on, then pop over to Pophams. Sacks of flour packed high along the walls announce the bakery – here you can enjoy your cappuccino while watching the artisan bakers craft delicious mango custard Danishes.

LUMBERJACK

Map 5; 70 Camberwell Church Street, Camberwell;
///hobby.grew.valid; www.wearelumberjack.co.uk

Community is at the heart of everything here, be it the single origin coffee provided by Brixton roastery Assembly Coffee, the prints by local artists for sale or the baristas who'll happily offer tips on the best nearby pubs. Talking of baristas, Lumberjack is part of the London Reclaimed charity, which helps young people step into work.

» **Don't leave without** browsing the shop, where you'll find eco-friendly candles, fancy crisps and natural wine.

PANGEA CAFÉ

Map 2; 74 Commercial Street, Spitalfields; ///award.ever.mull;
www.pangeacafé.com

Pangea is known colloquially as the "café in the suit shop" because, well, it's found in a suit shop. The brainchild of a forward-thinking 20-something Aussie, it's all about sustainability – from the beans through to the cups. There's even bags of compost up for grabs.

MONMOUTH COFFEE

Map 1; 27 Monmouth Street, Covent Garden; ///camp.normal.play;
www.monmouthcoffee.co.uk

Every caffeine-addicted Londoner knows Monmouth. Having started in the basement here in 1978, the roastery has become a household name, with branches across the city. But weary workers keep returning to the tiny original for perfect coffee and small talk with the baristas.

Liked by the locals

"The last decade has been an exciting one for London's speciality coffee. The bar for what constitutes great coffee is now so much higher here, meaning you can stumble upon exceptional coffee in all sorts of unexpected places."

RICHARD FRAZIER,
CHIEF MARKETING OFFICER AT WORKSHOP COFFEE

WORKSHOP COFFEE

**Map 1; 1 Barrett Street, Marylebone; ///suffice.drew.exile;
www.workshopcoffee.com**

Some places just know how to do coffee right. Workshop's beans are
seasonally sourced in Africa and South America and roasted in East
London before they're brought here to this quiet nook in Marylebone.
Perfect for those wanting a moment of zen with their caffeine.

ALLPRESS ESPRESSO ROASTERY & CAFE

**Map 3; 55 Dalston Lane, Dalston; ///paint.badge.elder;
www.allpressespresso.com**

Watch a batch of Allpress beans complete the careful roasting
process in this joiners' factory-turned-roastery while you sip on a
delicious finished brew in the café area. Sun shining? Pair a flat
white with a newspaper in the leafy garden.

OMOTESANDO KOFFEE

**Map 1; 8 Newman Street, Fitzrovia; ///fish.narrow.crisis;
www.ooo-koffee.com**

Having started as a little-known one-man band in a rundown
tatami house in Tokyo, Omotesando now has a loyal tribe of chic
devotees. This is partly down to the uber-cool minimalism, partly
down to the creative coffees and partly down to the baristas who
treat customers like they've known them for years.

**» Don't leave without trying the kashi. These baked little custard
treats are like a cute cuboid take on French cannelés.**

Cocktail Joints

London's thirst for carefully crafted cocktails – and now mocktails – seems to be unquenchable. Handily, the city is peppered with tempting cocktail bars to suit every taste, occasion and budget.

LYANESS AT SEA CONTAINERS

Map 5; 20 Upper Ground, South Bank; ///fingernails.spray.basic; www.lyaness.com

Mixologist Ryan Chetiyawardana – also known as Mr Lyan – just can't stop winning awards, and it's easy to see why. At his flagship bar Lyaness, a chef's approach is taken to cocktail-mixing; Mr Lyan's team scours the planet for the most intriguing ingredients and distils them into truly memorable drinks. Sitting pretty by the Thames, this is the place to enjoy a one-of-a-kind cocktail with your favourite person.

FREUD

Map 1; 198 Shaftesbury Avenue, Covent Garden; ///thinks.alert.flats; www.freud.eu

Tucked below street level on hectic Shaftsbury Avenue, this refreshingly unpretentious bar is a favourite of those in the know. A far cry from the glitz of its surrounding area, Freud's has a faded industrial feel – its bare concrete walls forming a blank canvas for a charged atmosphere, affordable cocktails and a rotating gallery of artworks. It's an intimate nook, the kind of place to bring a good friend or impress a date.

>> **Don't leave without** trying a gently egg-white-frothed, zesty-sweet Snow Queen cocktail – light and refreshing.

69 COLEBROOKE ROW

Map 2; 69 Colebrooke Row, Islington; ///people.stage.tamed; www.69colebrookerow.com

No one agrees on the name for this tiny, secretive bar. It's styled itself as "The Bar With No Name" but, given the lack of signage, for years people have simply called it 69 Colebrooke Row. What locals do agree on, though, is how good it is. Dimly lit and decked out with mid-century furnishings, this intimate bar hums with intellectual chatter as a sophisticated crowd sips on carefully crafted cocktails.

Shh!

While beloved boozer The Exmouth Arms is fit to bust every weekend night, no one seems to have cottoned on to the fact that there's a secret cocktail bar right upstairs; it's so secret that it doesn't even have a website. Climb the pub's narrow staircase up to 5CC, a candlelit bar littered with inviting leather seats. Espresso martinis are elegantly made by chirpy staff for friends toasting smugly to their choice of bar.

SPIRITLAND

Map 1; 9–10 Stable Street, Kings Cross; ///trial.punks.posed;
www.spiritland.com

This dimly lit wine and cocktail bar is a music lover's heaven, its
world-class sound system and mixing decks standing centre stage.
The music's a bit too loud for a casual chat, but most people are
here anyway to revel in the electronic sounds of DJs that would
normally sell out much bigger stages. Listen to the addictive beats
and absorb the intimate vibe while sipping on a deftly mixed cold
brew negroni or refreshing pisco punch.

THREE EIGHT FOUR

Map 5; 384 Coldharbour Lane, Brixton; ///venues.fear.soft;
www.threeeightfour.com

This is classic date territory: exposed plasterboard and brick walls,
dim caged lighting and the atmospheric buzz of spirited chatter
filling the intimate space. You'll probably need to book to get you
and your plus one past the metal-grilled stable doors – it's a

Try it!
MIX YOUR OWN DRINKS

London Cocktail Club *(www.london
cocktailclub.co.uk)* is known for daring,
playful cocktails. Learn from the maestros
at a cocktail-making masterclass, where
you'll craft three drinks in a session.

seriously popular spot – but once you're in you can drink your way around the experimental cocktail list and unusual selection of wines and beers. Thankfully there are also small plates to soak up the booze.

SATAN'S WHISKERS

Map 5; 343 Cambridge Heath Road, Bethnal Green;
///noon.cowboy.joins; www.satanswhiskers.com

Yes, some regulars might jokingly refer to a night here as "going to hell" but it was Satan's Whiskers that, in 2013, first sparked Bethnal Green's cocktail scene. Beyond the bar's dingy exterior, tempting cocktails are mixed for a decent price (around £7.50 a pop) and the menu changes daily, so there's always something new to try. Add in red-hot hip hop beats and you've got a devilishly good Friday night.

» Don't leave without continuing down the road to cocktail bar Coupette for a decadent champagne piña colada.

UNTITLED

Map 3; 538 Kingsland Road, Dalston; ///activism.pass.spine;
www.untitled-bar.com

Rockstar mixologist Tony Conigliaro is the man to thank for the menu at this uber-creative spot, which is modelled on Andy Warhol's Silver Factory in New York. Okay, this Dalston copycat is verging on pretentious – the sparse décor is fifty shades of polished-concrete grey, with tin foil-plastered walls. But the cocktails themselves are works of alchemy, using some pretty surprising ingredients (like the Snow cocktail, which is mixed with chalk vodka and white clay).

Beer Gardens

Few things beat the atmosphere of a London beer garden in the summer. Given even just a glimmer of sunshine and the city's pub patios – from riverside terraces to vast and buzzing yards – come alive.

DUKE OF EDINBURGH

Map 5; 204 Ferndale Road, Brixton; ///smiles.exit.rift; www.dukeofedinburghpub.com

Tucked away from the chaos of central Brixton, the Duke of Edinburgh's vast beer garden is a welcome oasis. It's a chilled spot that, despite its size, always gets packed. Trains rumble past as groups stake their claim on the large communal tables, ready for a long afternoon of chat fuelled by local beers. When hunger strikes, the White Men Can't Jerk street food hut is handily right next to the outdoor bar.

THE SHIP

Map 4; 41 Jews Road, Wandsworth; ///warns.picked.title; www.theship.co.uk

For southwest Londoners, sunny weekends in the city mean one thing: long, boozy days in The Ship's beer garden. Despite being rather oddly slapped in a heavily industrial part of Wandsworth, The Ship's been a go-to since 1786. It's all about the outdoors here:

a big beer garden on the banks of the Thames, lined with long communal tables. Sports fans, rejoice: there's also a handful of heated booths each with their own TV.

» Don't leave without ordering a pint of locally brewed Wandle ale, which is named after the nearby River Wandle.

THE MAGIC GARDEN
Map 4; 231 Battersea Park Road, Battersea; ///dates.grit.tulip; www.magicgardenpub.com

Festival-goers feel right at home in this Battersea boozer. Its back garden is full of quirky bohemian opulence: painted vines creep along its walls, fairy lights drape overhead and a tented roof creates an indoor-outdoor tipi area dotted with sunken sofas and vintage armchairs. The Magic Garden is well known for hosting live music and its stage even transforms into a banging dance floor as the night goes on. Who needs Glasto, really?

THE WHITE HART
Map 3; 69 Stoke Newington High Street, Stoke Newington; ///purely.value.slice; www.whitehart stokenewington.com

You'd never know that this imposing townhouse pub has the area's biggest secret garden out back. Make your way through the football-watching crowds clamouring at the bar and out the back to a huge green space dotted with picnic benches and strung with fairy lights. It's a down-to-earth beer garden that's not quite succumbed to the area's gentrification. If you're peckish, the pub grub is pretty solid, too.

THE PROSPECT OF WHITBY

Map 6; 57 Wapping Wall, Wapping; ///blocks.rooms.video;
www.greeneking-pubs.co.uk

A swaying willow tree, the lapping waters of the Thames, centuries' old charm; it's little wonder this Wapping beer garden is a favourite. The flagstone floors of London's oldest riverside pub have borne witness to everyone from pirates and sailors to East End criminals – there's even a hangman's noose dangling ominously outside. Today, the drinking den channels an altogether more welcoming vibe...

THE ALBION

Map 1; 10 Thornhill Road, Barnsbury; ///jazz.late.chew;
www.the-albion.co.uk

Once upon a time, this flower-fronted gastropub was the watering hole of farmers and Londoners escaping the city to rural Islington. Today, the polluted thoroughfare of Upper Street is just down the

Shh!

Few know West Hampstead's Bohemia House (*www. bohemiahouse.london*) so its leafy beer garden remains a well-kept secret. The clubhouse was used by Czech and Slovak immigrants after World War II, many of whom had fought alongside the Allied Forces. Order a pint of Czech beer at the bar, where the barman will tell you more of the club's history, before enjoying your drink outside on the grass.

road, but you can still get a taste of the country in the pub's tree-filled, wisteria-adorned back garden. City life feels a million miles away as you sip on a draught beer and bask in the sunshine.

PEOPLE'S PARK TAVERN

Map 3; 360 Victoria Park Road, Hackney; ///envy.scope.monks; www. peoplesparktavern.pub

Sprawling Victoria Park was created in 1845 for the ordinary people of the East End, earning it the moniker the People's Park. And this park-side tavern was given its name for the same reason. Beloved in the neighbourhood, it's the kind of place that caters to your every whim, whether that's a slap-up Sunday roast, a weeknight quiz or simply a kick-ass G&T to be sipped in the hacienda-style beer garden – one of London's largest, dotted with pastel-painted huts.

>> Don't leave without trying the Mangolicious pale ale courtesy of the pub's microbrewery, the Brew Lab.

THE GIPSY MOTH

Map 6; 60 Greenwich Church Street, Greenwich; ///deaf.keen.snacks; www.thegipsymothgreenwich.co.uk

Few beer gardens are watched over by a 19th-century tea clipper. Having crossed the river by the Greenwich Foot Tunnel or disembarked from one of the DLR stops, you'll find the Gipsy Moth pub is right there to welcome you. You can't miss it: it's right beside the *Cutty Sark*. Join jolly day-trippers and Greenwich residents sharing bottles of wine while you take in the ship in all its majestic glory.

Rooftop Bars

London's rooftops range from slick skyscraper spots to grungy converted car parks. We love them all, and the way that each area's personality shines through to a sunset backdrop of iconic views.

QUEEN OF HOXTON

Map 2; 1–5 Curtain Road, Shoreditch; ///forest.tender.fade; www.queenofhoxton.com

The Queen of Hoxton is a local favourite, thanks to its wild party nights, and the rooftop is its crowning glory. It's redecorated with a new theme every season, from a 1900s Parisian salon to a Japanese-style cherry blossom garden. Come winter, a huge tepee keeps punters warm while they enjoy mulled cocktails and skyline views.

FRANK'S

Map 5; 10th floor, multistorey car park, 95a Rye Lane, Peckham; ///thinks.overnight.lined; www.boldtendencies.com

Peckham's worst-kept secret, Frank's is a local icon. Atop a multistorey car park, Frank's opens to a mixed crowd of edgy locals and edgier art students each summer. There are installations to check out (the bar is part of a local not-for-profit arts organization), cocktails to toast with

If Frank's is busy, head to the rooftop bar atop the Bussey Building. You'll find the Rooftop Film Club here, too. and small plates to chow down on. The real draw, however, is the views: Londoners can't resist an evening here, lingering over an Aperol Spritz as the sun sets.

DALSTON ROOFPARK

Map 3; 18–22 Ashwin Street, Dalston;///chair.stuck.silly; www.dalstonroofpark.com

Only seasoned locals find their way, down an alleyway and up a metal flight of steps, to Dalston's one and only rooftop bar – an astroturfed suntrap, dotted with scenesters lounging on bean bags. Here, craft beers are sipped and juicy burgers (including veggie and vegan options) are devoured to irresistible beats.

» Don't leave without checking out the rotating, socially minded exhibition gallery, downstairs in the Print House Gallery.

BIG CHILL HOUSE

Map 1; 257–9 Pentonville Road, Kings Cross; ///cape.sadly.trim; www.bigchillbar.com

You could drink many a pint in this huge and rambling townhouse, famed for its DJ nights, without stumbling upon its roof terrace. Swing by between Monday and Thursday for happy hour (with an Aperol Spritz £5 and beers just £3), from 4 and 7pm. Buy you and your pals a round at the beach shack vending station before sunning yourselves in the reclining chairs. You'll feel like you're in more tropical climes, not frantic central London.

NETIL360

Map 3; 1 Westgate Street, London Fields; ///action.claps.jacket;
www.netil360.com

It's hard to believe this place is anything more than a multistorey car park as you climb up its seemingly endless concrete stairs. But step breathlessly onto the rooftop and you'll see why Netil360 is such a hit with the cool kids. You can see far and wide – from the Shard to the Gherkin to Canary Wharf – and the complete absence of seats means you and your party can sprawl across the astroturf.

QUEEN ELIZABETH HALL ROOF GARDEN

Map 5; Queen Elizabeth Hall, South Bank; ///prompting.notice.reader;
www.southbankcentre.co.uk

When the sun shines there's only one place Londoners have in mind: the South Bank. And where do they catch the last of the sun's rays? The hidden roof garden. Ascend the sunshine-yellow staircase to this oasis and sprawl amid the wildflowers and vegetable plots.

» **Don't leave without** donating online. The roof garden is tended to by a group of volunteers who have experienced addiction, homelessness or mental health problems.

TAMESIS DOCK

Map 5; Albert Embankment, Lambeth; ///rods.lion.traps; www.tdock.co.uk

Okay, this bar is technically on the rooftop of a barge rather than a building, but it's too good to miss. Moored between Lambeth and Vauxhall bridges, the 1930s Dutch barge has gorgeous views of the

Houses of Parliament. Bevvies are reasonably priced and – here's the clincher – there's free live gigs. It's first come first served, so make a beeline here early on a sunny day and enjoy the rough-and-ready vibe within earshot of Big Ben.

PRINCE OF WALES

Map 5; 467–9 Brixton Road, Brixton; ///cure.narrow.member;
www.pow-london.com

Sat atop the Prince of Wales' pub and club, this vast two-tier roof terrace hosts a series of marathon 12-hour parties throughout the summer. It's popular with young Brixtonians plus those drawn from further afield. When the sun's blazing, and you're surrounded by your friends, there are few better places to dance and drink the day away. The rooftop views perhaps aren't the best that London has to offer but you'll be having too much fun to care.

Shh!

Rooftop bars aren't just for summer. Skylight, above Tobacco Dock (*www.tobacco docklondon.com*), is at its best in winter, when you can pair a drink with a skate around its adorable ice rink. Forget the rinks at Somerset House and the Natural History Museum – the queues here are smaller, and the views are better, making for a memorable date night. But, if summer's your season, Skylight offers a croquet course during warmer months, perfect for you and your pals.

Cosy Pubs

Is there any institution more central to London than the pub? We think not. Nothing is better on a dreary day, when the sun's hiding and all you want is a cosy armchair, a log fire and a glass of something.

THE SPANIARDS INN

Map 6; Spaniards Road, Hampstead; ///tags.deeply.bossy; www.thespaniardshampstead.co.uk

The Spaniards exudes all the character you'd expect from one of London's oldest inns. The pub has been a Hampstead favourite since 1585 and counts poet Keats among its former regulars. These days, it's the definition of cosy: dogs doze beside their owners, cask ales are enjoyed with hearty roasts, and in the winter the scent of wood smoke drifts from the crackling fire. Perfect after a walk on the heath.

THE ROYAL OAK

Map 2; 73 Columbia Road, Bethnal Green; ///valid.social.leap; www.royaloaklondon.com

Spend a Sunday afternoon roaming along Columbia Road Flower Market and you'll be in full need of a classic, East End pint of ale. This old-school boozer has got you, cramming thirsty punters into its boisterous downstairs bar (more sedate guests head upstairs). Scour the room for a rickety stool or chair and crowd in with the rest of the regulars, who will always make room for a newcomer.

YE OLDE CHESHIRE CHEESE

Map 1; 145 Fleet Street, Temple; ///point.track.resist; 020 7353 6170

Every Londoner knows of Ye Olde Cheshire Cheese, which was rebuilt after the Great Fire of 1666. It's best known for its literary associations – Charles Dickens and Mark Twain were both known to sip on flagons of ale in the pub's warren of dark, low-ceilinged cellar rooms. There's no end of secluded corners to tuck yourself away in, perfect for a date. It's also run by the Samuel Smith Old Brewery, which means that its real ales come at best-value prices.

» **Don't leave without** seeking out the taxidermic remains of Polly the Parrot, the pub's foul-mouthed feathered resident, who died in 1926.

THE HARP

Map 1; 47 Chandos Place, Covent Garden; ///humans.smoke.blues;
www.harpcoventgarden.com

On a wet and dreary London evening, there are few sights more inviting than the illuminated stained-glass windows of this little London haven. Inside, the welcome is just as warm: squeeze in among the other punters lining the bar and let the genuinely knowledgeable bartenders recommend you a real ale (or two). There's little chance of a seat, but who needs one? Stick close to the bar for good chat and even better beer. It'll be last orders before you know it.

Solo, Pair, Crowd

No matter where you are in the city, you're never far from a classic London pub to get snug in.

FLYING SOLO
Get cosy in an old haunt
The King William IV in Hampstead village has been drawing locals in for 200 years and counting. Draw up a bar stool, order a pint and chat to the barmen – they have many a story to tell.

IN A PAIR
Romantic night for two
Nestle down with a bottle of red on one of the low sofas at The Windmill on Clapham Common. Fingers crossed in-house pup Max joins you both for a snuggle, too.

FOR A CROWD
Catch-up by the riverside
Grab your friends and nab a window spot at Wapping's Captain Kidd. This low-ceilinged riverside pub has lovely views over the Thames, there's always plenty of space and the drinks prices are a steal – perfect for a get-together.

THE DEVONSHIRE

Map 6; 39 Balham High Road, Balham; ///prime.feared.guess; www.devonshirebalham.co.uk

It might be big but, in the bleak mid-winter, The Devonshire is utterly snug. Order a pint of bitter, sink down in one of the chesterfields and keep your fingers crossed that local brass band Dat Brass arrives for a performance. You'll be warmed up and on your feet in no time.

» Don't leave without popping in of a Sunday and sharing a Beef Wellington, followed by sticky toffee pud.

THE IVY HOUSE

Map 5; 40 Stuart Road, Nunhead; ///quick.gums.feel; www.ivyhousenunhead.com

When this pub building faced demolition in 2013, the good folk of Nunhead clubbed together to save their beloved local. Now cooperatively owned, the people's pub hosts a bevy of pint-fueled knitting circles, book clubs and pub quizzes.

THE PALM TREE

Map 3; 127 Grove Road, Mile End; ///woes.trials.posed; 020 8980 2918

Standing stalwart on the canal, this boozer is one of the last remaining to enjoy a proper Cockney knees-up. The décor has little changed in 50 years, likewise the drinks choice hasn't evolved, and the owners still haven't set up a website. Still, every Friday and Saturday night, locals congregate for live crooning jazz (just wait for Kerry the barmaid to take the mic) and the pub feels like a home away from home.

Breweries and Distilleries

Yes, London's a city that has long loved drinking booze but it's also one that loves making it. And a growing wave of distilleries and urban wineries are stealing the limelight from beloved craft breweries.

BULLFINCH BREWERY

Map 5; Arches 886–7 Rosendale Road, Herne Hill; ///stud.deep.cages; www.thebullfinchbrewery.co.uk

Set in a railway arch near Brockwell Park, wonderfully unpretentious Bullfinch Brewery will give you all the local community feels; punters shift up to make space, dogs obligingly let you tickle their tummies and the person who'll pull your pint most likely brewed it.

KANPAI

Map 5; Unit 2A.2, Copeland Park, 133 Copeland Road, Peckham; ///roses.speeds.spins; www.kanpai.london

Something special has been quietly brewing away in the shadow of Peckham's much loved Bussey Building. The UK's first sake brewery is set in a tiny warehouse; you'll spot the puffs of steam from its fermentation tanks, the warehouse doors flung open whatever the weather. In winter, punters in beanies and thick scarves huddle over steaming bowls of ramen and sip their hot sake; in the summer they spill out onto the pavement with glasses of refreshingly cold sake. Learn all about the art of the Japanese drink on a Saturday brewery tour.

» Don't leave without trying a glass of sparkling sake – few people know that this Japanese spirit also comes in a crisp, bubbling form.

HAWKES CIDERY AND TAP ROOM
**Map 5; 90 Druid Street, Bermondsey; ///funny.swim.fancy;
www.wearehawkes.com**

Nestled amid the craft ale sellers on the Bermondsey Beer Mile, Hawkes is something different from its neighbours. For one, it's London's first urban cidery. Add to that the fact that it crafts ciders from donated apples and those rejected by supermarkets and you'll see why eco-conscious Londoners love it. The handmade stone-baked pizzas are also a welcome sight for boozy punters.

Shh!

Off the beaten path, and away from the crowds thronging along Bermondsey Beer Mile, is Walthamstow Beer Mile. Little known, even among Londoners, there's a wonderful neighbourhood community feel in the taprooms here. Breweries includes award-winning Pillar, Wild Card, Exhale and Signature, with more expected to open as hype grows.

BERMONDSEY DISTILLERY

Map 5; 55 Stanworth Street, Bermondsey; ///heats.chest.bands;
www.bermondseygin.com

A place that's confidently not trying to do anything new, Bermondsey
Distillery is a love letter to the past. Inspired by London's lost distilleries,
this small-batch place is devoted to traditional gin botanicals.
Under the arches by Maltby Street Market, it opens on weekends
for those wanting to stretch out their market visit with something a
little stronger. Gin aficionados should check out the distillery tours.

EAST LONDON LIQUOR COMPANY

Map 3; 221 Grove Road, Bow; ///goal.props.teams;
www.eastlondonliquorcompany.com

In 1903, the Lea Valley Distillery became the last East London
whisky maker to turn off its stills, ending the long history of distilling
in the area. Today, this small producer of whisky, gin, vodka and rum
has reinstated those spirit-making roots. Based in a former glue
factory by the canal in Bow Wharf, the on-site tasting bar always
has plenty of seats and a chilled vibe.

CRATE BREWERY

Map 6; Unit 7, Queens Yard, Hackney; ///gone.panels.fund;
www.cratebrewery.com

Crate is a cavernous former print factory with craft beers on tap,
industrial canalside views, and a sea of beards and tattoos; yes, this
place is peak hipster but it pulls it off well. On sunny days, crowds

Earn your pint by kayaking to Crate with Secret Adventures. Trips on the canal start at Limehouse Basin.

sprawl along the canalside – sharing jugs of beer and rounds of pizza – as narrow-boats tootle past and the DJ hits their stride. There's nowhere better to be.

HACKNEY CHURCH BREW CO.
Map 3; 16–17 Bohemia Place, Hackney; ///first.bound.glass;
www.hackneychurchbrew.co

It might be little but this Hackney brewpub packs a punch. The on-tap brews span crisp IPAs to chocolatey stouts, all designed to please the palates of Hackney's famous craft beer addicts. Better yet, most of the brewing ingredients are sourced within a stone's throw of the brewery, showing off its community focus. You won't want to spill a single drop.

RENEGADE LONDON WINERY
Map 2; Arch 12, Gales Gardens, Bethnal Green; ///moving.silves.shark;
www.renegadelondonwine.com

London's concrete jungle isn't the first place you'd think to open a winery but as the English wine scene blossoms, urban wineries are starting to pop up here. Renegade, East London's first winery, turns the best grapes from England and Europe into experimental new blends. Its wine bar, set in a graffiti-sprayed railway arch dotted with candlelit tables, barrels and fermentation tanks, is a brilliant place to sample its produce. On balmy nights head to the lovely outdoor terrace for a glass or two.

CITY OF
LONDON

BANKSIDE

Admire the view from
THE OLD THAMESIDE INN
This former spice warehouse was
converted into an inn, its position by the
Thames ideal for delivering goods. Sip a
pint here and enjoy the riverside locale.

1

Thames

TOOLEY STREET

PARK ST

ST THOMAS STREET

2

Soak up history at
THE GEORGE INN
Stop by the city's only surviving
coaching inn – which dates
back to medieval times – to
admire its galleried façade
and tuck into a hearty pie.

DRUID STREET

JAMAICA ROAD

3

Snoop around at
JENSEN'S GIN
DISTILLERY
Bermondsey was "London's Larder"
in the 19th century, storing produce
in its many warehouses. Today
Jensen's uses one for the distillation
of gin, based on an 1840s recipe.
Take a tour to find out more.

BERMONDSE

ENID STREET

LUCEY W

SOUTHWARK PARK RL

0 metres 500
0 yards 500

An afternoon of
brewing history

This is a city built on brewing. The 18th century saw the development of a dark, hoppy beer called porter – so-called because river porters used to enjoy it – which made London the UK's main brewing city. Production increased and Southwark, just south of the Thames, became a central hub of beer-making. Despite a decline in brewers in the 1900s, London has seen a boom since the noughties, with some of the city's best artisanal breweries and distilleries centred in Bermondsey, right next door to Southwark.

Bermondsey Beer Mile *perfectly embodies London's modern craft beer revolution. The stretch of microbreweries opens on Saturdays.*

Pop into PARTIZAN
Partizan has been brewing since 2012. Grab a table in its makeshift tap room and round off your tour with a zesty double-hopped IPA.

SHADWELL

WAPPING

SOUTH BERMONDSEY

1. The Old Thameside Inn
Pickfords Wharf, Borough;
www.nicholsonspubs.co.uk;
///pencil.bunch.organ

2. The George Inn
75–7 Borough High Street, Southwark;
www.greeneking-pubs.co.uk;
///tuned.region.tulip

3. Jensen's Gin Distillery
55 Stanworth Street, Bermondsey; www.bermondseygin.com;
///buns.camera.dreams

4. Partizan
34 Raymouth Road, Bermondsey; www.partizanbrewing.co.uk;
///most.cherry.sprint

Bermondsey Beer Mile
///brief.less.feel

SHOP

Shopping is woven into the lives of Londoners: markets shape weekends, vintage boutiques update wardrobes and book nooks offer the next gripping read for the commute.

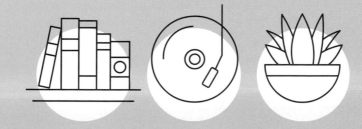

Vintage Gems

London has long loved vintage, and the retro revolution continues to make waves. Stalwarts of the scene, like Portobello Market, are now rivalled by an abundance of second-hand emporiums.

ALADDIN'S CAVE

Map 6; 72 Loampit Hill, Lewisham; ///punch.peanut.truly; 020 8320 2553

This crumbling former railway station is one of London's more bizarre shopping experiences. Furniture explodes onto the pavement – wicker chairs, time-worn sofas and claw-foot bathtubs – all making a bid to escape the clutches of this eclectic store. Inside, items are stacked to the ceiling, blocking out the daylight.

ALFIES ANTIQUES MARKET

Map 4; 13–25 Church Street, Marylebone; ///chain.monday.slimy; www.alfiesantiques.com

We can't talk about London's vintage scene and not mention Alfies, a labyrinthine marketplace based in an old Art Deco department store. Here almost 100 expert dealers care for their wares – polishing-19th century silverware, preening 1920s dresses and rearranging mid-century furniture.

OLD SPITALFIELDS MARKET

Map 2; 16 Horner Square, Shoreditch; ///fetch.herb.engine;
www.oldspitalfieldsmarket.com

Old Spitalfields, East London's original market, might be hemmed in with gleaming stores but the locals keep coming back for all its knick-knacks. Here, geezers in flat caps and cool kids in bucket hats rummage in unison through vintage maps and dog-eared books.

PORTOBELLO ROAD MARKET

Map 4; Portobello Road, Notting Hill; ///bath.raced.models;
www.portobelloroad.co.uk

Pretty pastel-hued buildings, vintage dresses swaying in the breeze, the lyrical cries of traders to throngs of eagle-eyed shoppers; visiting Portobello Road is a quintessential London activity. Saturdays are liveliest, with what feels like most of the city pouring over the pre-loved curiosities that fill the rickety market tables.

» Don't leave without seeing the Banksy mural near the corner of Portobello Road and Acklam Road.

ROYAL TRINITY HOSPICE

Map 4; 27 Kensington Church Street, Kensington; ///down.landed.often;
www.royaltrinityhospice.london/kensington

Designer garms for a good cause are the name of the game at this boujee charity shop, where impeccable Christian Dior pieces hang from the rails and near-perfect Manolo Blahniks line the shelves. Come to replenish your wardrobe with some timeless pieces.

PAPER DRESS VINTAGE

Map 3; 352a Mare Street, Hackney; ///rocket.fund.insert;
www.paperdressvintage.co.uk

This sustainable boutique by Hackney Central station goes by the simple mantra: clothing from the past was built to last, so why waste your money on fast fashion? Pop in to browse vintage garb spanning the 20th century, with retro-styled staff on hand to help you find your look. Come nighttime, platform heels are swapped for trainers when the shop is transformed into a live music and event space.

BEYOND RETRO

Map 3; 92–100 Stoke Newington Road, Dalston; ///king.that.system;
www.beyondretro.com

Whichever area of London you're in, you'll see groups of teens and 20-somethings decked out in 1990s athleisure wear, pre-loved aviator jackets and vibrantly patterned headscarves. Chances are these fashion gems were picked up at Beyond Retro, a name revered by London's vintage shoppers. This particular treasure trove

Try it!
FASHION FIX UP

Got a pair of vintage jeans that need a little TLC? Get your stitch on at Fabrications on Broadway Market. The shop runs various upcycling and garment repair workshops with the friendliest crafting experts.

has more than 12,000 unique pieces, from sparkly flapper dresses to retro American sweaters. You won't be able to get away without at least one plaid shirt – you've been warned.

>> **Don't leave without** checking out the shop's reworked vintage range. The fit or style has been retailored to match modern runway trends.

ANNIE'S

Map 2; 12 Camden Passage, Islington; ///tested.member.march;
www.anniesvintageclothing.co.uk

Annie's is the doyenne of London's vintage shopping, attracting serious fashionistas in search of old-world glamour (Kate Moss frequents this jewel of a store). Beautifully curated and with an air of decadence, this is the place to unearth the wedding dress of your dreams or a gown for a fancy work event. There's also a bargain rail for those who want to leave with a little piece of vintage for just a few pounds.

BRICK LANE VINTAGE MARKET

Map 2; 85 Brick Lane, Shoreditch; ///feel.points.clear;
www.vintage-market.co.uk

East London and vintage shopping go hand in hand, thanks to the area's wonderfully rich history and its famously creative residents. Just look at The Old Truman Brewery – once the city's largest brewery and today the home of Brick Lane Vintage Market. Every day of the week, stallholders with an eye for style cram their vintage wares into the weathered warehouse, with hipsters quick to comb the rails for feather capes, leather jackets and dapper suits.

Record Shops

London is a city rippling with musical history, and this is celebrated in its record shops. Surely there is nothing more rewarding than unearthing an elusive album or dusting off a classic vinyl to take home?

LITTLE RECORD SHOP

Map 6; 43 Tottenham Lane, Crouch End; ///clouds.racks.spit; www.cash4records.co.uk

You're in safe hands at this North London gem, where vinyl collector David has been buying and selling records for over 15 years. Here you'll find rare collections of prog rock, folk, 1950s jazz, northern soul, funk, post-punk — whatever you're hankering after, he's got it. Better still, he offers fairer prices than you'll find elsewhere. Join other music fans in making this your number-one calling point.

AUDIO GOLD

Map 6; 308–10 Park Road, Muswell Hill; ///prompting.surely.twice; www.audiogold.co.uk

Audio Gold by name and by nature; this Muswell Hill haven is the place to visit if you're getting into vinyl or looking to upgrade. Few other places have such a chocolate box of audio equipment, starting with wind-up gramophones and extending to second-hand hi-fis from the 1980s and 1990s – the heyday of musical manufacturing. Make use of the staff's sage advice and try out anything before you buy.

» Don't leave without scanning the room for UK music royalty; BBC radio regulars in particular love Audio Gold.

ROUGH TRADE EAST

Map 2; Truman Brewery, Brick Lane; ///exit.turned.supply; www.roughtrade.com

The Rough Trade label became a household name among UK musos when it signed The Smiths in the early 1980s. Now, it's known for this vast record store and gig space, where a purpose-built stage hosts album debuts. The range of CDs and vinyl on offer is huge: you'll come for your favourite band's latest release and leave hours later with three or four other records in tow that you never knew you needed. It's a must-visit for anyone exploring Brick Lane.

Shh!

Keep an eye out for the Rough Trade gig listings *(www.roughtrade.com/gb/events)*. Entry is usually free with the purchase of the album that's being promoted, and though sets are shorter than in bigger gig spaces, they're much more intimate. Some unexpectedly big names have performed here, too; Radiohead played a surprise six-song set in 2008. Who will be the next big band or artist to perform?

FLASHBACK RECORDS

Map 2; 50 Essex Road, Islington; ///clear.rider.tries; www.flashback.co.uk

Seasoned rockers and young ravers unite at the entrance to Flashback, wooed by the bargain buckets of records by the front door. Pass through the ground floor dedicated to CDs and find the vinyl-only room downstairs, where you'll see serious music fans search for unique samples of rare jazz, hip hop and soul. There's even another branch of Flashback Records on Brick Lane if you need a second hit.

» Don't leave without enquiring about the store's events programme, dedicated to the artists signed to the Flashback Records label.

RECKLESS RECORDS

Map 1; 30 Berwick Street, Soho; ///shared.ranged.piles; www.reckless.co.uk

Nostalgia calls at this family-run shop, which has been buying and selling small record collections for over 40 years. After a bit of 1960s prog? They've got it. Drum and bass more your thing? That's here too. In short: this place has a pleasing amount of everything. It's hardly surprising that music lovers adore it; after all, it even featured on the cover of Oasis album *(What's the Story) Morning Glory?*

PHONICA

Map 1; 51 Poland Street, Soho; ///rats.finely.stores; www.phonicarecords.com

Movers and shakers gravitate toward this dance vinyl specialist, where stacks of minimal techno and nu disco are flaunted beside dubstep and French electro – arguably, the shop's most impressive section. Speak to the uber-cool staff about the Phonica Records label, Record Store Day parties and live streams – all different ways to worship at the altar of dance music. You might even find yourself next to DJ regulars Four Tet, Floating Points or Caribou.

MUSIC AND VIDEO EXCHANGE

Map 4; 38 Notting Hill Gate, Notting Hill; ///trails.cases.reward;
www.mgeshops.com

Since 1967 this place has been categorizing and flogging crates of pre-loved vinyl records and CDs. The Exchange is constantly unearthing well-thumbed records to sell on, which means an ever-evolving stock; a selection you see on a Monday could be completely different by Friday. This means two things: you must snap up a bargain the moment you see it, and you must come back to visit as often as possible. You won't be the only one – some hardcore regulars at this shop come back several times a day.

KRISTINA RECORDS

Map 3; 194 Well Street, Homerton; ///each.plant.scales;
www.kristinarecords.com

This independent crate-diggers' haven based in South Hackney specializes in weird and wonderful avant-garde releases. The whole vibe is cool and modern, which beckons to younger music fans who are on the hunt for dance music gems or a new set of mixing decks. The staff are uber knowledgeable and more than happy to recommend a record or two; you'll find yourself picking their brains over a coffee in the shop café.

Book Nooks

Bookshops are cornerstones of their neighbourhoods: beautifully curated shops where children's first books are bought, cosy corners offer refuge and travel adventures are dreamed up.

DAUNT BOOKS

Map 1; 83–4 Marylebone High Street, Marylebone; ///supporter.hardly.entry; www.dauntbooks.co.uk

Edwardian store Daunts is the most beautiful place to browse: soaring ceilings, ornate windows and row upon row of tomes. It's not strictly a travel bookshop but has long been seen as a travel specialist; the stacks of guidebooks will spark wanderlust in the most casual browser.

RYE BOOKS

Map 5; 47 North Cross Road, East Dulwich; ///milky.cute.forgot; www.ryebooks.co.uk

Blink and you could miss Rye Books but you really don't want to. An expertly curated selection of books line the walls, labradoodle George snoozes by the counter and the smell of freshly brewed coffee fills the air. The lovely staff are also founts of bookish knowledge and are only too happy to recommend a delicious read for your journey home.

GAY'S THE WORD

Map 1; 66 Marchmont Street, Bloomsbury; ///packet.lanes.tennis; www.gaystheword.co.uk

This was the UK's first gay and lesbian bookstore when it opened in 1979 and continues to stand proud. A dedicated LGBTQ+ following love Gay's The Word for its prize-winning fiction and cutting-edge queer theory. There's also a busy calendar of inclusive discussion groups and events that adds to the community spirit.

WORD ON THE WATER

Map 1; Regent's Canal Towpath, Kings Cross; ///exists.gazed.junior; www.wordonthewater.co.uk

Bobbing on the Regent's Canal amid the rejuvenated grit of King's Cross, this wonderfully quirky floating bookshop is an unmissable spot for bookworms. The 1920s Dutch barge is packed with old and new books, crammed onto its deck and smuggled into its hull.

» Don't leave without checking out upcoming events: bookish discussions, live music, open-mic nights and slam poetry evenings.

STANFORDS

Map 1; 7 Mercer Walk, Covent Garden; ///stable.marble.couple; www.stanfords.co.uk

We admit it, we're biased, but it's hard to resist a bookshop dedicated to travel, adventure and escapism. Since it was established in 1853, Stanfords has become the go-to destination for backpackers researching their next adventure and armchair travellers alike.

Liked by the locals

"Burley Fisher is a community. We run regular events and stock a lot of books and zines by small and independent publishers. Online stores may be convenient, but it will never replicate the pleasure of browsing a well-curated bookshop."

SAM FISHER, CO-FOUNDER AT BURLEY FISHER BOOKS

LIBRERIA

Map 2; 65 Hanbury Street, Shoreditch; ///clap.bets.export; www.libreria.io

A stone's throw from the hurly-burly of Brick Lane, Libreria is a welcome refuge for readers, who come to peruse the floor-to-ceiling shelves of modern fiction, poetry and biographies. Some regular customers even curl up in the shop's little cubbyholes, which are built into the bookshelves, to read a few pages before buying.

» Don't leave without asking the sales assistant to stamp your chosen book with "Libreria" at the till.

NEW BEACON BOOKS

Map 6; 76 Stroud Green Road, Finsbury Park; ///handy.owners.dent; www.newbeaconbooks.com

In 2017 the local community rallied around this bookshop, raising funds to save it from closure and protect it from the onslaught of the digital age. It's a place worth treasuring – this was the UK's first Black bookshop when it opened in 1966, and has been celebrating African and Caribbean voices and literature ever since.

BURLEY FISHER BOOKS

Map 3; 400 Kingsland Road, Dalston; ///atom.ants.nature; www.burleyfisherbooks.com

Edgy East Enders study tomes through their round tortoise-shell glasses at this indie treasure trove. It's all about small-press books and community spirit at Burley Fisher, which is best experienced with a glass of red at a literary event in the popular basement bar.

Home Touches

Londoners love personalizing their homes, whether that's with a jungle of plants, jazzily coloured soft furnishings or locally crafted pottery. And you can buy a bit of London to take home too.

FOREST

Map 5; Rear of 43 Lordship Lane, East Dulwich;///ticket.parade.slurs; www.forest.london

You'd struggle to find a Londoner who doesn't have a luscious fern or pot of ivy draped across their desk or window sill. Those living south of the river turn to Forest — a tiny, tropical nook of a plant shop packed with little armies of cacti and succulents waiting patiently for a new home. And if you can't pack a plant, don't fret; there's a beautiful collection of lifestyle products tucked amid the greenery.

CHOOSING KEEPING

Map 1; 21 Tower Street, Covent Garden; ///windy.ideal.tulip; www.choosingkeeping.com

There's no temple to the art of stationery quite like Choosing Keeping, which is named to reflect the kind of stationery that is carefully chosen and kept for years to come. The serenely organized shop is awash with Tuscan marbled notebooks, gold-nib fountain pens, ceramic pen holders, Japanese pencils, decorative paperweights – everything you could possibly need for kitting out your home office.

NUNHEAD GARDENER

Map 5; 1a Oakdale Road, Nunhead; ///nods.simply.filled; www.thenunheadgardener.com

Run by Peter Milne and his husband Alex Beltran, who both quit their city jobs to follow their true passion for plants, the Nunhead Gardener is not your run-of-the-mill garden centre. In these two railway archways green-fingered retirees hobnob with trendy young professionals, all foraging through the succulents, cacti and glazed pots for something to brighten their homes.

» Don't leave without strolling up the hill for a walk through the eerily beautiful, forested pathways of Nunhead Cemetery.

Shh!

A house isn't a home without great art on your walls – or so says Mimi, the bubbly owner behind Mimi V Artworks *(81 Balham High Road)*. Tucked away at the tail end of Balham High Road, this art gallery and framing shop is a true gem. Mimi takes pride in her window displays, which showcase works by local artists and, inside, staff offer top advice on anything you want framed. Oh, and dogs are most welcome.

CORNERCOPIA

Map 6; 63 Streatham Hill, Streatham; ///views.jars.dwell;
www.cornercopiastore.co.uk

Cornercopia is like a rustic home, with its shelves of gorgeous – and often locally made – homeware items (think lambswool blankets and hand-crafted wooden utensils). And what else does a home need? A snoozing pet, of course. Say hello to Ginger the cat while you're here.

» Don't leave without browsing the enticing homeware collection in boutique store Lark, just down the hill from Cornercopia.

RACHEL AND MALIKA'S

Map 5; Unit 38, Granville Arcade, Brixton; ///fits.towns.weedy;
www.rachelandmalikas.com;

What started as a shop dedicated to instruments from Mali is now a celebration of crafts from around the globe. Owners Kat and Malika curate sustainable, artisan home goods from women's co-ops and economically poor communities. It's impossible to pass by without stopping to admire the gorgeous rugs and woven baskets that pour out of the shop.

GOD'S OWN JUNKYARD

Map 6; Unit 12, Ravenswood Industrial Estate, Shernall Street,
Walthamstow; ///themes.intent.nets; www.godsownjunkyard.co.uk

This psychedelic store is a must-visit, whether or not you're in the market for some neon home lighting. Accessed via a nondescript car park, God's Own Junkyard is truly eye-watering, thanks to the vintage neon street signs, disco balls and kitsch memorabilia that cover every single surface. You can feel a bit woozy in all that neon glare; fortunately the in-house coffee shop is at arm's length – perfect for regaining your balance over a brew.

THE CONRAN SHOP

Map 1; 55 Marylebone High Street, Marylebone; ///soak.cross.entry; www.conranshop.co.uk

Expect to mingle with a well-dressed clientele in this iconic London homeware store. The Conran Shop is renowned for its colourful collections of swanky homeware that hit all the current design and homeware trends. Even if you're just casually browsing the cushions, glassware, candles or stationery, something will make its way into your shopping basket; you've been warned.

CONSERVATORY ARCHIVES

Map 3; 493–5 Hackney Road, Hackney; ///fall.broke.rather; www.conservatoryarchives.co.uk

Vast windows, faded tiles and bare plaster walls form the backdrop to the main event here: a jungle of tropical plants. When it opened in 2015, Conservatory Archives was the first indoor plant store in the UK, spearheading a growing obsession with adopting plant babies for our homes. Interspersed with mid-20th-century furniture, a lush tangle of greenery greets visitors: foliage-draped hanging baskets, the sprawling leaves of cheese plants and row upon row of bulbous succulents. It's all great fodder for a social media feed.

Beloved Markets

London's markets are at the core of city life. From crack-of-dawn butchers supplying restaurants to weekend markets where locals browse artisan goods, these city stalwarts keep the capital humming.

BROADWAY MARKET

Map 3; Broadway Market, London Fields; ///shirts.sketch.wished; www.broadwaymarket.co.uk

On Saturdays this Hackney street houses London's hippest market. A fruit and veg market has been on the site since the 1890s, and food is still the main draw — young families and groups of flatmates browse the artisan cheeses, baked goods and mounds of fresh produce to take home. Food aside, there's plenty else to buy, from vintage clothes to fresh blooms to handmade crafts.

COLUMBIA ROAD FLOWER MARKET

Map 2; Columbia Road, Hackney; ///afford.love.petty; www.columbiaroad.info

For many Londoners, Columbia Road is the perfect Sunday day out and a remaining slice of East London, where the sing-song of traders' cockney rhyming slang rings out above the crowds. Sure, some will recommend you arrive early to beat the rush, but we say where's the fun in that? Hit the street at midday, coffee in hand from a local independent, and shuffle along with the rest of them, pausing to treat yourself to a bouquet of beautiful blooms.

» **Don't leave without** stocking up on pots for your leafy purchases from the brilliantly named Stoned & Plastered, just off Columbia Road.

SMITHFIELDS MEAT MARKET

Map 2; Charterhouse Street, City of London; ///rich.owner.supper;
www.smithfieldmarket.com

Housed in three listed buildings, this is the largest wholesale meat market in the UK. Things kick off early here, with the gates swinging open at 2am on weekdays to savvy restaurateurs, city butchers and meat-fiends with an eye for a bargain. In the moonlight the market hums: white-cloaked porters frantically steer rattling pallet trucks and the jovial banter of long-time traders fills the air.

BROCKLEY MARKET

Map 6; Lewisham College car park, Brockley; ///paying.loans.entire;
www.brockleymarket.com

Every Saturday a humble car park is transformed into one of London's best farmers' markets. Fresh produce abounds — mounds of organic fruit and veg, stacks of cheese and glistening fish. Young couples flock here, as do families with pushchairs and dogs looking longingly at the butcher's counter. Browse the stalls, sampling as you go, but leave space for lunch from one of the street food trucks.

Solo, Pair, Crowd

Barter best alone? Fancy hitting the stalls with some friends? There's a London market to suit every need.

FLYING SOLO

A bloom of one's own

Set your alarm early and make your way down to Battersea for the New Covent Garden Flower Market. Things kick off at 4am (every day bar Sunday) but the bargain blooms make the early start worth it.

IN A PAIR

Village vibes and private picnics

Browse Greenwich Market's *(p40)* bustling stalls and grab some street food or picnic supplies before popping over to wonderfully leafy Greenwich Park. The views across the Thames aren't too terrible, either.

FOR A CROWD

Market goods and rooftop booze

London's hippest market, Broadway Market is the perfect place for a group exploration – finish up with rooftop views and drinks at nearby Netil360 *(p70)*.

BRIXTON VILLAGE AND MARKET ROW

Map 5; Atlantic Road, Brixton; ///teach.evenly.cape;
www.brixtonvillage.com

Straddling the frenetic scene of Atlantic Road are Brixton Village and Market Row, a duo of covered markets that symbolize the soul of Black Britain. Gentrification has seen pizza places and chichi boutiques replace much-loved family-run Afro-Caribbean stores; this is London with all its complexities. Forgo the chains and show your support to the original and Black-owned small businesses.

CAMDEN MARKET

Map 1; Camden Lock Place; ///highs.latter.puzzle; www.camdenmarket.com

You can't miss this market – it's under a huge "The Camden Market" sign. Before that you'll see crowds of grungy teens and bearded hipsters thronging along Camden Lock, looking to spend their money on vintage clothing, quirky art, Gothic jewellery and more besides.

SOUTH BANK BOOK MARKET

Map 5; under Waterloo Bridge, South Bank;
///punt.boxer.duck; www.southbanklondon.com

Of course a city with long literary traditions needs a market dedicated to the written word. Every day, commuters and pals meeting for dinner stop under the shade of Waterloo Bridge to peruse the rows of tables lined with second-hand novels, maps and comics.

» Don't leave without popping into the British Film Institute (BFI) Riverfront Bar to make a start on your new read with a glass of wine.

An afternoon of
vintage shopping

Once the poorest quarter of the city, East London is today the most creative – you only need to look at the locals' fashion to realize. The likes of Shoreditch and Spitalfields are breeding grounds for well-priced vintage stores selling pre-loved vinyl, clothing and homeware. Start on Brick Lane, featuring one of the most renowned clusters of second-hand vendors in the UK, before walking up to Hackney and finishing the day with some pints at a classic East End boozer.

1. Poppie's
6-8 Hanbury Street,
Spitalfields; www.poppies
fishandchips.co.uk;
///clocks.both.wiring

2. Brick Lane Vintage Market
85 Brick Lane, Shoreditch;
www.vintage-market.co.uk;
///feels.points.clear

3. Rough Trade East
91 Brick Lane, Shoreditch;
www.roughtrade.com;
///exit.turned.supply

4. Rokit
101/107 Brick Lane,
Shoreditch; www.rokit.co.uk;
///tones.polite.live

5. The Birdcage
80 Columbia Road,
Hackney; www.draft
house.co.uk;
///rank.spit.highs

The Well and Bucket
///dragon.mime.grant

HOXTON

OLD STREET

GREAT EASTERN STREET

Liverpool Street
Station

BISHOPSGATE

Columbia Road, *today a haven for vintage shops, was once home to a food market for the poor set up by philanthropist Angela Burdett-Coutts in 1896.*

Ion Square Gardens

5 **Rest your feet at THE BIRDCAGE**

Order a drink in the historical Birdcage, or "The Birdy" to locals. If you're lucky, you might even catch a live gig.

COLUMBIA RD

COLUMBIA RD

VIRGINIA ROAD

SWANFIELD STREET

BETHNAL GREEN ROAD

Weaver's Fields

Standing stalwart, **The Well and Bucket** *is one of the East End's oldest pubs, having first opened in 1818. The tiling inside shows the pub's age.*

SHOREDITCH HIGH STREET

SHOREDITCH

SCLATER ST

CHESHIRE ST

BRICK LANE

Make a detour to ROUGH TRADE EAST

Electronica fan? Prefer punk, or funk? Whatever music you like, chances are you'll find it in Rough Trade East's vintage vinyl section.

4 **Pop into ROKIT**

You'll find a bargain at Rokit, like a second-hand denim jacket or perhaps an 80s jumpsuit.

3

2 **Peruse the rails at BRICK LANE VINTAGE MARKET**

Try on pre-loved Doc Martens and military-style coats at this indoor market, where vintage specialists sell clothing from the 1920s onwards.

1 HANBURY ST

SPITALFIELDS

BISHOPSGATE

Lunch at POPPIE'S

Grab a table by the jukebox and tuck into a parcel of fish and chips at this white-tiled, family-run chippie.

BRICK LANE

WHITECHAPEL

ARTS & CULTURE

London is a cultural colossus. Cavernous museums tell the vital stories of the past, while indie galleries and striking street murals comment on the present and future.

City History

The UK and its capital have been shaped by people, so it should only follow that its museums celebrate the richness of our shared past. These small but mighty institutions are a great starting point.

LONDON TRANSPORT MUSEUM

Map 1; Covent Garden Piazza, Covent Garden; ///that.overnight.goad; www.ltmuseum.co.uk

Buried beneath London is another world: sealed-off Tube stations, crumbling tunnels and abandoned platforms. It's a world that the young families enthusiastically exploring the old Tubes and buses here know nothing about. Impress your own parents and book onto the museum's exclusive Hidden London tours, where you'll uncover lost spaces, such as bomb shelters used by Londoners in World War II.

MUSEUM OF LONDON DOCKLANDS

Map 6; 1 Warehouse, West India Quay, Canary Wharf; ///puppy.sweep. ranged; www.museumoflondon.org.uk

The West India Docks were the world's largest dock complex when they opened in 1802 and this museum, in the shadow of skyscrapers, looks at how these historical warehouses operated. Here you'll discover

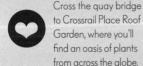 Cross the quay bridge to Crossrail Place Roof Garden, where you'll find an oasis of plants from across the globe. | the stories of merchants and pirates, the trade of enslaved African people and sugar, and the uncomfortable resulting success of the British economy and empire.

THE POSTAL MUSEUM

Map 1; 15–20 Phoenix Place, Clerkenwell; ///being.orange.vouch;
www.postalmuseum.org

Okay, a visit to a postal museum doesn't sound like the most exciting of days out but this sorting office genuinely brings to life five fascinating centuries of postal work in the city. Learn how Royal Mail grew from a handful of messengers who delivered notes from the king into an integral nationwide service. The true highlight is the chance to ride on the city's secret postal railway, a 100-year-old subterranean train that transported packages and letters across the capital.

» Don't leave without grabbing a bite to eat at foodie-favourite Exmouth Market, which is a mere five-minute walk away.

THE JEWISH MUSEUM

Map 1; 129–31 Albert Street, Camden; ///limes.format.dizzy;
www.jewishmuseum.org.uk

East London was traditionally the heartland of Jewish settlement in the UK though today communities live in all corners of the city. Set in a townhouse in Camden, this expansive museum reflects the experiences of Jewish Londoners and houses important Holocaust and anti-racist exhibitions.

DENNIS SEVERS' HOUSE

Map 2; 18 Folgate Street, Spitalfields; ///dine.ants.panel;
www.dennissevershouse.co.uk

London has long been a city of immigrants. Take the French Huguenots, who moved en masse to then-affordable Spitalfields in the 17th century. Artist Dennis Severs transports you to that time at 18 Folgate Street with an intimate imagined portrait of family life. It's adults only and particularly popular with cuddled-up couples.

BLACK HISTORY WALK

Map 2; Tower Hill underground station, Tower Hill; ///year.space.goats;
www.blackhistorywalks.co.uk

Brush up on London's often-ignored Black history by booking yourself and your friends onto a Black History Walk. Designed by founder Tony Warner, the walks – which cover 12 areas of the city – bring a more

Shh!

Want to see London from a different perspective? Unseen Tours *(www.unseentours.org.uk)* do just this, highlighting the hidden stories and secrets around the likes of Shoreditch, Soho and Covent Garden. Even better, this is a social enterprise with tours led by formerly homeless Londoners. You could explore Shoreditch with Henri the humorist, Soho with knowledgeable Nic or Covent Garden with "Vive-pedia." (Seriously, Viv knows everything about the local area.)

rounded world-view to the many London tours on offer. We suggest the Black History Walk in Tower Hamlets to get you started; you'll learn all about London Docklands' history of slavery before ending up at the Museum of London Docklands (p108).

THE NATIONAL COVID MEMORIAL WALL

Map 5; start at Westminster Bridge, Albert Embankment, South Bank; ///baked.lease.bland; www. nationalcovidmemorialwall.org

In March 2021, after the worst of the COVID-19 pandemic, a group of volunteers painted 150,000 hearts on a 500-m (1,640-ft) stretch of wall facing the Houses of Parliament. They encouraged bereaved families from across the UK to fill these hearts with the names of loved ones tragically lost to the virus. More hearts and names have been added since, making the London wall a moving symbol of the country's collective grief and a reminder of what was lost. It's a must-see.

EAST END WOMEN'S MUSEUM

Map 6; Abbey Green, Barking; www.eastendwomensmuseum.org

In 2015, a proposed women's history museum in East London instead opened as a museum dedicated to serial killer Jack the Ripper. Uproar ensued, culminating in a Kickstarter campaign to fund this museum, which is dedicated to the telling of women's stories via exhibitions, events and workshops. The museum is opening in a brand new space in Barking in 2023; visit with your girlfriends and celebrate girl power.

» Don't leave without getting the inside line on monuments to women's history that can be visited across London.

Public Art

London has long been home to colour-splashed streets. From famous pieces by graffiti giants to ever-evolving tunnels where newer artists practise their craft – there's always something different to see.

LEAKE STREET TUNNEL

**Map 5; Leake Street, Waterloo; ///quest.energetic.rested;
www.leakestreetarches.london**

The constantly changing Leake Street Tunnel is one of the best spots to catch street art in the making. Since Banksy put it on the map with the 2008 Festival of the Cans, this 300-m (984-ft) tunnel has become a go-to for practising artists, especially taggers who paint joyful pieces that you'll want to snap and share. The tunnel is transformed from day to day – usually a fresh piece of work from the morning will already have been sprayed over by nightfall.

RIVINGTON STREET

Map 2; Rivington Street, Shoreditch; ///moves.owls.impose

The first thing you notice on a visit to Shoreditch is the paint-splattered streets. In fact, there's such a wealth of it that it can be hard to know where to begin. To see the best of it, head to Rivington Street, where

The Shoreditch Street Art Tours are a great way to see more (*www.shoreditch streetarttours.co.uk*).

you'll see the stick figures synonymous with local artist Stik and the striking *Scary* mural by Eine, which is intended to poke fun at those who fear graffiti.

BRICK LANE

Map 2; Brick Lane, Shoreditch; ///trades.walk.custom

The bricks of Brick Lane have many stories to tell: Bengali street signs signal the area's history of immigration, peeling posters hint at political leanings and street murals provide a social commentary. A tour here gives a great snapshot of local life. After all, London's hoi polloi love to meander here, stopping on their day's errands to take in longstanding artworks by urban art legends D-Face, ROA and Omar Hassan and those by newer artists looking for their big break.

» Don't leave without pausing mid-tour for a drink in Montys Bar, surrounded by vivid murals on all sides.

PORTOBELLO WALL
PUBLIC ART PROJECT

Map 4: Portobello Road, Portobello; ///forum.senior.shape

Since 2009, an unassuming brick wall connecting two West London roads (Portobello Road and Golborne Road) has been transformed into an outdoor gallery. Every year the 100-m (328-ft) stretch is mounted with works by a local artist that celebrate the area's people and culture. Previous years have seen displays such as Connections, an expo of portraits of Portobello locals by artist Anastasia Russa.

BRIXTON STREET ART
Map 5; Brixton; ///pink.anyone.crowned

Brixton is home to some of South London's best and most politicized urban art. Here you'll discover works from the 1970s and 80s as well as modern anti-gentrification pieces. The Save the Brixton Arches campaign, established in 2015, united street artists who supported local businesses battling eviction from the railway arches along Atlantic Road. Grab a coffee and visit early in the morning, when the shop shutters are down, revealing these powerful artworks.

» Don't leave without checking out the David Bowie mural on Tunstall Road, just around the corner from the singer's birthplace.

KENTISH TOWN ROAD
Map 1; Kentish Town Road, Camden; ///chained.claps.views

One of the best pockets of Camden's famous street art lives in Kentish Town Road. Here, bold and abstract murals give Camdenites in their ubiquitous Doc Martens reason to pause as they go about their business. Their favourite mural? That's the unmissable portrait of local icon Amy Winehouse on Camden Road.

FISH ISLAND
Map 6; Fish Island, Hackney; ///uses.flight.call

Fish Island is dotted with artist's studios but many taggers prefer to create on the streets, with Stour and Smeed roads both great starting points for admiring their work. Want to see taggers hard at work with their spray cans? The towpath at Hertford Union Lock is a good bet.

Liked by the locals

"Street art and graffiti are essential to our society. They're a form of expression that gives everyone and anyone an opportunity to have their views heard – political and social. It's a vital medium of expression, and London more than anywhere else has really embraced that."

USAMAH KISE, STREET ARTIST

Favourite Museums

Thanks to their fame, London's encyclopaedic museums can get crowded. But there are ways to experience these cultural powerhouses in relative peace and with a difference.

NATURAL HISTORY MUSEUM

Map 4; Cromwell Road, South Kensington; ///encounter.poems.magic; www.nhm.ac.uk

While wide-eyed schoolkids might rule the roost during the day, this beloved museum is for adults only when dusk falls. The monthly Lates are something special: DJs entertain below the entrance hall's vast blue whale skeleton, food and drink stalls pepper the corridors and exhibitions – like the must-see Wildlife Photographer of the Year – can be enjoyed without having to elbow people out the way.

TATE MODERN

Map 5; Bankside, Southwark; ///sparks.expert.thinks; www.tate.org.uk

For gallery veterans marking the weekend and arts newbies looking for some culture on a Friday night, Tate Modern's Lates have become a popular fixture in the calendar. Taking place on the final Friday of the month, these free events bring together and celebrate creativity in all its forms, with banging tunes, challenging artworks and fun workshops. Of course, this is also the ideal opportunity to have a peek at the world-class modern art collection.

V&A

**Map 4; Cromwell Road, South Kensington; ///boats.cards.hint;
www.vam.ac.uk**

Stylish, fashion-forward Londoners love the Victoria and Albert Museum. This design powerhouse has hosted sell-out exhibitions dedicated to wedding dresses, underwear and kimonos, plus creations by Christian Dior and Alexander McQueen. The free Lates, on the last Friday of the month, are a chance to delve behind the permanent displays, with visitors egged on to participate in performances, live installations and debates.

NATIONAL GALLERY

**Map 1; Trafalgar Square, Charing Cross; ///rice.common.silver;
www.nationalgallery.org.uk**

This world-class collection opened in 1824 with the intention of bringing art to everybody. This ethos lives on now more than ever; it's free entry and there are daily talks covering everything from medieval portraiture to French Impressionism. Then there are the Friday night Lates, film screenings and music performances. Why shouldn't Van Gogh's *Sunflowers* brighten everybody's day?

» Don't leave without checking out the Talk and Draw events, where you're invited to sketch an artwork after an introduction to its origins.

Solo, Pair, Crowd

A day in London without a slice of culture is unthinkable, but there's always a way to get your fix.

FLYING SOLO
Walk and talk

Familiarize yourself with London's history, and make friends en route, on a Museum of London walking tour. Topics include the Great Fire of London and local queer history. Find out more online.

IN A PAIR
Giggle with a date

Get past the first date awkwardness by joining a life-drawing class. The London Drawing Group offer pay-what-you-wish classes at the National Gallery.

FOR A CROWD
Disco with dinosaurs

London's most unusual setting for a silent disco is the Natural History Museum's striking Hintz Hall. Here you and your mates can dance the night away under the suspended skeleton of Hope, the mascot blue whale.

TATE BRITAIN

Map 4; Millbank, Westminster; ///files.robe.native; www.tate.org.uk

She might be overshadowed in popular opinion by her cool younger sister but, blimey, Tate Britain has a lot to offer. Like your art romantic? You'll love the Pre-Raphaelites. Prefer brighter paintings? Look out for David Hockney's works. Want to really immerse yourself in art? Check out the Late sessions, which are wonderfully community focused.

BRITISH MUSEUM

Map 1; Great Russell Street, Bloomsbury; ///unfair.purple.echo; www.britishmuseum.org

The British Museum was the first national museum anywhere in the world to be open to the public and that spirit of inclusivity remains today, with free exhibitions every day of the week (as well as ticketed ones) and 20-minute spotlight tours on Fridays.

» Don't leave without checking out the controversial Parthenon Sculptures, which continue to spark debate about the legitimacy of removing cultural treasures from their homeland.

SCIENCE MUSEUM

Map 4; Exhibition Road, South Kensington; ///film.ozone.matter; www.sciencemuseum.org.uk

On the last Wednesday of the month, the museum opens for adult-only, booze-friendly nights. Expect to get hands-on with science and ask all the big questions like "Could I survive an apocalypse?" and "Is my phone controlling my love life?"

Indie Galleries

This is a city that loves to push the boundaries, especially when it comes to art. Paintings, photography, installations: all are showcased in the most weird and wonderful spaces.

THE CRYPT GALLERY

Map 1; St Pancras Church, Euston; ///bids.crab.foil; www.cryptgallery.org

In the early 1800s, departed Londoners were buried in church crypts rather than overcrowded graveyards. That was outlawed in 1854, but the crypt at St Pancras Church had already interred 557 bodies. Their remains now watch over one of London's most atmospheric and macabre gallery spaces, where sound installations and art shows are erected among the underground stone alcoves and archways.

180 THE STRAND

Map 1; 180 The Strand, Strand; ///opera.fairly.cloud; www.180thestrand.com

This Brutalist icon is home to one of London's most exciting creative centres. Having launched in 2016, the complex houses the likes of vinyl-pressing enterprise and record label The Vinyl Factory, alternative media group Dazed and music magazine *Fact*. These

 While you're here, pop into Somerset House, which holds various exhibitions *(www. somersethouse.org.uk)*. creatives throw open their doors for some of the city's sexiest exhibitions, attracting art students and local office workers looking for a culture fix.

THE PHOTOGRAPHERS' GALLERY

Map 1; 16–18 Ramillies Street, Soho; ///forks.laptop.home;
www.thephotographersgallery.org.uk

Moved from various locations to this refitted old brick building, tucked behind Oxford Circus, this was the UK's first public gallery dedicated to the photographic arts – with a mission to promote the medium as one of our most significant artforms. As such, the classy space is a creative hub for all things photographic: exhibitions, yes, but also talks and events with London's art glitterati.

» Don't leave without visiting the bookshop, which stocks utterly gorgeous photography tomes – perfect for updating your coffee table.

WHITE CUBE

Map 5; 144–52 Bermondsey Street, Bermondsey; ///duty.scan.drum;
www.whitecube.com

In 1993, a tiny, square room in the art-dealing corner of the West End became a solo exhibition space with a rule that an artist could only be exhibited once. There many young British artists – such as Tracey Emin and Sarah Lucas – held career-changing shows. After an 11-year stint in Hoxton, the White Cube resides in Bermondsey and remains the go-to place for free-thinkers who worship conceptual art.

SAATCHI GALLERY

Map 4; Duke of York's HQ, King's Road, Chelsea; ///copy.boots.looked;
www.saatchigallery.com

Much like the White Cube, this gallery became synonymous with young British artists in the 1990s, thanks to the promotion of talents like Hirst and Emin by Iraqi-British businessman Charles Saatchi. Today chic aficionados and wannabe art critics flock to the uber-cool Saatchi Gallery, keen to see the next big names in British art.

THE OLD POLICE STATION

Map 6; 114–16 Amersham Vale, Deptford; ///solid.renew.happy;
www.lewisham.gov.uk/organizations/the-old-police-station

Have you ever been chin-stroking over an artwork and had to sidestep the toilet bowl that's blocking your view? This former police station-turned-gallery in New Cross might be the only place in the world where that's a real possibility. Ex-holding cells, busted open but with

When good-timers pile off the carriage at Hackney Downs station on a Saturday, little do they know there's an indie gallery right there on platform 1. Banner Repeater is a contemporary and experimental art space, dedicated to developing art in a commuter station (*www.banner repeater.org*). You don't need to buy a ticket — though if you're disembarking be sure to tap out your payment card first.

their latrines intact, have been converted into intimate exhibition spaces, while shipping containers outside house artist studios. The whole place has a DIY mindset, with artists collaborating on projects.

» **Don't leave without** grabbing a hot mulled cider at kitsch cocktail bar Little Nan's, next door to Deptford station.

NOW GALLERY

Map 6; Peninsula Square, Greenwich; ///admiral.hunt.handed; www.nowgallery.co.uk

Looking to find the next big artist? Look no further. In the shadow of the Millennium Dome O2 Arena, this modern space is dedicated to representing a whole host of backgrounds and career levels in its art, fashion, photography and design shows. Two exhibitions return annually to promote young, diverse talent: Human Stories, a photographic series that unpicks social constructs around race and identity; and a Young Artist showcase to spotlight emerging talent.

CAMDEN ART CENTRE

Map 6; Arkwright Road, Hampstead; ///stem.slot.pies; www.camdenartcentre.org

Not many tourists make it to Finchley Road, the busy stretch that extends from Regent's Park to Hampstead. But those that do are rewarded with this quiet and pleasant contemporary art space – a hidden gem that would draw much bigger crowds if they only knew it was here. The gallery also has a secret-garden café that draws local lunch-breakers craving its big slabs of quiche.

Get Crafty

Sometimes the best way to get to know a city, and the people who call it home, is to get hands on. Londoners love their crafts – whether handling cool clay, hot candle wax, just-cut blooms or neon pastels.

POTTERY AT THE KILN ROOMS

Map 5; Unit 202 Level 2, Peckham town centre car park, 95A Rye Lane, Peckham; ///reform.smiled.likes; www.thekilnrooms.com

Former multistorey car park Peckham Levels has been transformed into a hotbed for local talent, showcasing Peckham's small creative businesses. For the pottery-curious, the Kiln Rooms' five-hour taster sessions let you try your hand at clay work and create a few pieces of your own to be fire glazed. The perfect date activity (think *Ghost*).

Try it!
CRAFTIVISM

Keep an eye out for compassionate protests that use knitting and cross-stitching to convey anti-capitalist, environmental or feminist messages. Check out events with Craftivist Collective *(www.craftivist-collective.com)*.

THE FLOWER APPRECIATION SOCIETY

**Map 3; BE Studios, 72A Southgate Road, Hackney; ///harp.barks.tribe;
www.theflowerappreciationsociety.co.uk**

This floral studio hums with the chatter of girlfriends celebrating a
birthday or bride-to-be. Run by two sisters who grow many of the
blooms around the corner in an urban cutting garden, workshops
cover everything from bridal bouquets to Christmas wreaths.

» Don't leave without buying a copy of A to Z of All Things Floral
to keep crafty when you're back home.

SOCIAL POTTERY

**Map 6; 120 Kentish Town Road, Kentish Town; ///fries.baking.press;
www.socialpottery.com**

There's something meditative about painting – less so when you've
got all your mates around you and a gin tin in hand (it's BYO).
Choose from hundreds of pottery pieces – mugs, jugs, bowls, pots –
plus paints and stencils, and embrace your inner Picasso.

MODERN CALLIGRAPHY AT
VINTAGE HEAVEN

**Map 2; 82 Columbia Road, Hackney; ///foods.scarcely.shout;
www.alicegabb.com**

Been roped into writing your best friend's wedding invites? Lettering
artist Alice Gabb is here to help with her calligraphy workshops. Alice
supplies all the worksheets and words of wisdom you could possibly
need, and the lovely folk of Vintage Heaven are on hand with cake.

CLAY WORK SESSIONS AT KANA

Map 3; 5A Gransden Avenue, London Fields; ///glass.flag.mason;
www.kanalondon.com

There's an individuality to Ana Kerin's handmade ceramics – the ghost of a subtle imperfection, the trace of a fingertip on the glaze, the echo of a hand across the surface. Tableware lovers should keep their eyes peeled for her workshops, where you can learn her hand-crafted, wheel-free style, with classes on everything from mug making to crafting your own crockery.

LONDON TERRARIUMS

Map 5; 106A New Cross Road, New Cross; ///couch.priced.delay;
www.londonterrariums.com

Londoners' unquenchable thirst for bringing greenery into their homes doesn't look set to slow down any time soon. For anyone who struggles to keep their plant babies alive, terrariums are the perfect low maintenance option. Check out terrarium making classes at London Terrariums, where you can craft your own self-contained tiny ecosystem of ferns, ivy and soft moss.

CANDLEMAKING AT EARL OF EAST

Map 3; 5 Gransden Avenue, Hackney; ///dock.tests.kite;
www.earlofeast.com

Warm Atlas cedar, the zing of Amalfi lemons, the faded smell of cigars that reminds you of your grandfather – scents can transport you to a place, person or memory. Crafting and preserving that nostalgic association in a candle is what the classes at Earl of East are all about. Learn to hand-pour your own soy wax candle in the magical scent lab before browsing the calming store, where class members get a 20 per cent discount.

NEON NAKED LIFE DRAWING
Map 2; 89 Great Eastern Street, Shoreditch; //assets.dinner.rival;
www.neonnaked.com

Art class meets Full Moon Party in this psychedelic life-drawing experience. Picture this: a dark room lit by UV lights, a model glowing in reactive body paints, your neon pastels following their movements around the room. Artist Jylle Navarro's background in fashion and performance inspired her to start these unique art classes, which take place at various locations, including in circus-inspired Trapeze Bar.

» **Don't leave without** heading down into Trapeze Bar for a drink and acro-balance or contortion performance after your class.

Kintsugi is the latest Japanese craft to be quietly making itself known among London's Japanophiles and pottery lovers. Using gold resin to weld together cracks in treasured pieces of crockery, Kintsugi revolves around the idea that the mended product – with its new and beautiful scars – is even more precious than the original item. Check out Indytute for workshop listings (www.indytute.com)

KNIGHTSBRIDGE

Explore the glorious V&A

This is the world's foremost art and design museum. Marvel at ancient ceramics, intricate wallpapers, and gorgeous theatre costumes.

4

BROMPTON ROAD

CROMWELL ROAD

THURLOE PLACE

BROMPTON ROAD

WALTON STREET

SOUTH KENSINGTON

A celebration of French culture, the Institut Français on Queensbery Place opened its doors in 1908. Its Ciné Lumière draws film lovers today.

OLD BROMPTON RD

5

Dine at DAPHNE'S

Devour delicious Italian fare – perhaps washed down with a glass of fizz – and admire the artworks that line the walls of this classy spot.

3

Lunch at DOZO

Restaurants don't get more stylish than Dozo. Grab a floor cushion, or *zabuton*, and order a Japanese bento box.

SLOANE AVE

ONSLOW GARDENS

SYDNEY STREET

CHELSEA

KING'S ROAD

KING'S ROAD

FULHAM ROAD

OLD CHURCH STREET

KING'S ROAD

In 1964, fashion designer Mary Quant created the world's first-ever miniskirt in her boutique at No. 138a King's Road.

2

Stock up on supplies at GREEN & STONE

Feeling inspired? Buy everything you need to create your own masterpiece at this old and creaky art materials shop.

0 metres   300
0 yards   300

A day ambling through
arty West London

From its roots as an artists' colony in the 19th century to its heyday as the centre of the Swinging Sixties in the 20th, the borough of Kensington and Chelsea has long been an enviable postcode in the art world. An abundance of designer boutiques, paint shops and local galleries have drawn many notable residents to this area (think J M W Turner and Mick Jagger) and, today, cultural Kensington and swanky Chelsea remain stomping grounds for fashionistas, art collectors and eager-eyed designers.

Start at
SAATCHI GALLERY
While away an hour or so at one of the world's most distinctive contemporary art centres before grabbing a coffee-to-go from the café.

1. Saatchi Gallery
King's Road, Chelsea;
www.saatchigallery.com;
///copy.boots.looked

2. Green & Stone
259 King's Road, Chelsea;
www.greenandstone.com;
///spine.woven.gloves

3. Dozo
68 Old Brompton Road,
South Kensington; www.
dozosushi.co.uk
///oasis.tops.actor

4. V&A
Cromwell Road, South
Kensington; www.vam.ac.uk;
///boats.cards.hint

5. Daphne's
112 Draycott Avenue,
Chelsea; www.daphnes-
restaurant.co.uk
///works.slim.gossip

Institut Français
///invite.raft.soccer

138a Kings Road
///tins.reach.lock

NIGHTLIFE

Whatever day of the week, London turns the volume up when darkness falls: groups descend on bustling food halls, musicians take to stages and revellers dance until dawn.

Evening Food Halls

Something of a misnomer, these places aren't just about food. Animated crowds of friends line communal benches, bop to great tunes and charge their glasses. It's as much about socializing as sustenance.

EATALY

Map 2; 135 Bishopsgate, Liverpool Street; ///maple.flies.field; www.eataly.co.uk

City slickers rejoiced when food emporium Eataly threw open its doors in 2021, immediately descending on the Liverpool Street marketplace to get their fill of Italian fare. And who can blame them? Replete with various cafés and restaurants, a drinking terrace (Aperol Spritz, anyone?) and mini Italian supermarket, there's

Try it!
COOK ITALIAN

We all want to master the art of prepping and cooking real Italian food and, thanks to Eataly, you can. The food hall hosts all manner of classes, including risotto and pasta-making workshops.

something to keep you busy and – more imporantly – well-fed every night of the week. And, when you're feeling fat, full and ready to roll home, Liverpool Street station is handily right next door.

FLAT IRON SQUARE

Map 5; 45 Southwark Street, Bermondsey; ///cones.edgy.swung; www.flatironsquare.co.uk

London's disused railway arches are forever being transformed into trendy watering holes and nightclubs, and those in Bermondsey are no exception. Under the rumble of trains pulling into London Bridge, Flat Iron Square hosts a buzzy taproom (with reliably good beats) and food stalls serving up gloriously carby pizzas, burgers and tacos. This place is no secret so book your group's spot well in advance.

» Don't leave without heading next door to Omeara *(p142)* for some live music and a dance once you've been fed and watered.

MODEL MARKET

Map 6; 196 Lewisham High Street, Lewisham; ///plans.parade.slower; www.streetfeast.com

Lucky it's open till 1am (Fridays and Saturdays) as you could easily spend a whole night here. It's a place to head en masse – bring your mates, and their mates, and make some new mates while you're here too – such is the party atmosphere. Yep, it's next to a tired-looking shopping centre but looks aren't everything. Expect to find a buzzing tequila bar, thumping soundtrack and treats from London street food royalty, like Fundi Pizza.

BOXPARK

Map 2; 2–10 Bethnal Green Road, Shoreditch; ///drip.ballots.flank;
www.boxpark.co.uk

Boxpark might be London's definitive pop-up market. Set in shipping containers opposite Shoreditch High Street train station, it's home to some of the city's best street food (don't miss the vegan eats from What the Pitta). This is the place to be seen; cool kids sip cocktails, snap photos and enjoy the beats spun by up-and-coming DJ talent, grime MCs and soulful house DJs.

MARE STREET MARKET

Map 3; 115 Mare Street, Hackney; ///donor.hobby.they;
www.marestreetmarket.com

Anything Shoreditch can do, Hackney can do better. Just look at Mare Street Market, a former job centre that has been transformed into an indoor food hall with a strict no-plastic policy. It's open every day of the week but it's especially buzzy on weekends, when trendy millennials decked out in athleisure wear descend in their droves to browse the market's delis and quaff locally brewed beers.

MERCATO METROPOLITANO

Map 5; 42 Newington Causeway, Elephant and Castle;
///people.rises.title; www.mercatometropolitano.com

Elephant and Castle isn't the most happening place, we'll be honest, but it does have Mercato Metropolitano. Open all day every day, the street food hub really comes into its own as dusk falls; the vast

There's another branch of Mercato – based in a truly beautiful deconsecrated church – in Mayfair.

rooms of stalls fill out with good-timers chatting over chewy-crusted pizzas and pints of beer. It's the perfect place for raucous evenings with all your loved ones.

POP BRIXTON

Map 5; 49 Brixton Station Road, Brixton; ///bridge.beyond.lamps; www.popbrixton.org

Vibey, loud and always packed, Pop Brixton is Brixton's go-to destination for foodie, boozy alfresco nights out. Two levels of colour-splashed shipping containers – dens for tiny eateries and bars – are packed with a young crowd, beers in hand, every night of the week. Music thumps in the background and the scent of fried food fills the air.

TOOTING MARKET

Map 6; 21–3 Tooting High Street, Tooting; ///shells.labs.straw; www.tootingmarket.com

For too long Brixton has held the limelight. Enter Tooting, a foodie's paradise with a lovely community feel. Come evening and Tooting Market is a hive of activity: families devour bowls of bubbling curry, students discuss politics over steaming ramen and professionals clink wine glasses. Can't spot a seat? Check out Tooting Broadway Market, just a short hop away.

» **Don't leave without** one last drink at Tap 13, a zero-waste tap bar with a great atmosphere in Tooting Broadway Market.

Game Night

Millennials are getting married and buying flats but the thought of growing old brings them out in hives. Luckily there's plenty of places to put their maturity aside and revel in a bit of friendly competition.

FLIGHT CLUB

Map 1; 55 New Oxford Street, Bloomsbury; ///crafty.study.judge; www.flightclubdarts.com

The humble game of darts has been drawn out of the shadows of old-school boozers and given a high-energy makeover. Everything about this place is fun: the noughties tunes, the tear-and-share pizza and, of course, the darts games themselves. Whether you're looking for a date night with a difference, or weekend tomfoolery with your London family, Flight Club won't let you down.

ELECTRIC SHUFFLE

Map 5; 10 Bermondsey Street, London Bridge; ///fall.labs.cotton; www.electricshuffle.com

The folks behind Flight Club have another ace up their sleeve: Electric Shuffle. Office workers can't get enough of this buzzy shuffleboard spot, letting off steam with competitive colleagues after a hard day's

After battling it out over the boards, refuel with Mexican street food (hello tacos) at Santo Remedio.

work. It's all fun and games until a feisty opponent knocks your disc off the board. Thankfully, strong cocktails are on-hand to cheer up even the sorest of losers.

THE CRYSTAL MAZE LIVE EXPERIENCE

Map 1; 22–32 Shaftesbury Avenue, Piccadilly; ///oldest.likes.super;
www.the-crystal-maze.com

We salute the wacky team that decided to resurrect 1990s game show *The Crystal Maze* in real life. The immersive game of mental, physical and skilfull challenges is overseen by an entertaining Maze Master, making for a very memorable birthday, hen or stag do. Tickets aren't cheap and it books up far in advance – but trust us, it's just about the most fun you will ever have.

» Don't leave without getting a photo in your iconic satin bomber jacket – you can even buy one to take home.

BALLIE BALLERSON

Map 2; 97–113 Curtain Road, Shoreditch; ///beard.minds.keen;
www.ballieballerson.com

Remember the pure, unadulterated joy of launching yourself into a ball pit? Relive those childhood memories at this Shoreditch playground for grown-ups, which features two ball pits and a ball pit waterfall. The excited shrieks of 20-somethings clowning around in the pits are accompanied by a banging soundtrack of R'n'B and disco beats. It makes for a night to remember.

ALL STAR LANES

Map 1; Victoria House, Bloomsbury Place, Holborn; ///worry.drew.duty; www.allstarlanes.co.uk

Relive the fun-filled birthdays of your childhood with an evening of bowling – this time washed down with beers and cocktails. Popular with groups of over-excited office workers looking to unwind after work, All Star Lanes even has a number of karaoke booths so you can make a proper night of it.

FOUR QUARTERS

Map 5; 187 Rye Lane, Peckham; ///codes.unwanted.modest; www.geocities.fourquartersbar.co.uk

Packed-out with retro consoles and arcade games, and set to the soundtrack of concentrated thumb tapping, this is where South London's hipsters come for a bout of gaming nostalgia. Evenings

Shh!

London has long had a thing for vintage arcade games so new kid on the block NQ64 is a welcome addition *(www.nq64. co.uk)*. The Soho bar is covered with fluorescent UV paint and churns out old-school hip hop. But you're here for the consoles, which range from arcade classics to GameCube and XBOX. And the games? There's Street Fighter II, Mortal Kombat, Star Wars pinball... basically, all you could possibly need for a raucously nerdy night out on the town.

are frittered away going square-eyed on Pac Man or battling it out in an intense gaming tournament. Whoever loses buys the next round of beers.

ROOF EAST

Map 6; Stratford multistorey car park, Great Eastern Way, Stratford; ///grades.translated.tower; www.roofeast.com

This place taps into not one but two of London's weaknesses – an insatiable thirst for rooftop bars and an obsession with transforming car parks into fun spaces. As soon as summer hits, grown-up city-dwellers scale the heights of Roof East to run riot at this playground. Dating duos flirt their way around the crazy golf, while mates battle it out in the batting cages – all fuelled by the ubiquitous craft beer and street food, of course.

JUNKYARD GOLF CLUB

Map 2; 88 Worship Street, Hackney; ///toward.lonely.grapes; www.junkyardgolfclub.co.uk

You wouldn't expect a weird and wonderful nine-hole golf course made from scrapyard slides and disused car parts to work, but it does. Especially with its array of cocktails served in red party cups and garnished with mini packs of Love Hearts sweets. Junkyard Golf is pure, unadulterated fun for big kids, so book in your mates and get putting to the beats of old-school hip hop.

» Don't leave without buying a bag of pick-n-mix; you'll get flashbacks to carefully choosing penny sweets in the corner shop as a kid.

Live Music

The Rolling Stones, Coldplay, Florence and the Machine, Stormzy – these music gods all started their careers here in London. And the city's venues continue to host incredible acts across all genres.

ROUNDHOUSE

Map 1; Chalk Farm Road, Camden Town; ///swear.relate.pushes; www.roundhouse.org.uk

Most Londoners will have heard of the Roundhouse, fewer will know why it's round: its circular shape dates back to when it was a railway engine repair shed. These days, it's one of London's most sacred venues and a beloved Camden landmark. Theatre, spoken word and circus shows are performed here but it's live music that lures young rockers and indie lovers in their droves.

THE HAGGERSTON

Map 3; 438 Kingsland Road, Dalston; ///bugs.loyal.early; 020 7923 3206

A topsy-turvy pub with a ramshackle back garden, this icon is remembered by longtime East Enders as Uncle Sam's, where Sunday-night jazz sessions would keep the party going until 3am. The management changed hands in 2008 but the jazz remained, and

Sate your appetite before or after the jazz with chicken tenders at Chick 'n' Sours, just next door.

it's still the safest bet for a memorable Sunday night out in East London. It can get rammed – the *feng shui* needs work – but the musical talent is rock solid.

UNION CHAPEL

Map 6; 19B Compton Terrace, Islington; ///number.tribe.author;
www.unionchapel.org.uk

How often have you cradled a cup of tea while watching a gig? A far cry from the booze-fuelled, jostling floors of many venues, the Union Chapel is a magical experience. Set in a Grade I-listed Gothic masterpiece, this is a calm space where a spellbound audience fills church pews. With its soaring acoustics and ornate stained-glass window forming a glowing backdrop, it's the perfect setting for stripped-back gigs.

JAZZ CAFE

Map 1; 5 Parkway, Camden Town; ///nodded.jolly.hulk;
www.thejazzcafelondon.com

In 2020 the Jazz Cafe celebrated 30 years as London's temple to hip hop, jazz, funk and soul, with royalty like Erykah Badu, D'Angelo, Amy Winehouse and The Pharcyde having all graced its stage. The 440-capacity venue hosts DJs and MCs for weekend shows, with cool Londoners busting serious moves to their beats.

» Don't leave without checking out the upstairs balcony, where you can book a dinner table with an uninterrupted view of the musicians.

EARTH

Map 3; 11–17 Stoke Newington Road, Dalston; ///demand.fool.humble;
www.earthhackney.co.uk

Locals were gutted when, in 2018, the iconically down-and-out Efes Snooker Club put down its cues for the last time. But in the building's place came EartH (Evolutionary Arts Hackney): an arts venue with a community-focused ethos and a line-up of new rap and jazz talent.
» Don't leave without pausing for a drink and a cultural chat with the locals on the first floor's secret garden terrace.

HOOTANANNY

Map 5; 95 Effra Road, Brixton; ///life.bake.insect;
www.hootanannybrixton.co.uk

A hootananny isn't just what Jools Holland gets up to on New Year's Eve; Brixton pub Hootananny is all about letting your hair down and savouring great live music. It's one of London's premier spots to see up-and-coming artists of a head-spinningly diverse range of genres.

OMEARA

Map 5; 6 O'Meara Street, London Bridge; ///mixed.prefer.sketch;
www.omearalondon.com

In an exposed-brick archway, Omeara is owned by Mumford & Sons' Ben Lovett but its gig offerings go way beyond the banjo-twanging folk rock that the London band is famed for. The venue has steadily become one of the top places to headhunt rap and grime artists, though come the weekend it's all about house and funk.

VILLAGE UNDERGROUND

Map 2; 54 Holywell Lane, Shoreditch; ///jelly.rust.pens;
www.villageunderground.co.uk

Londoners know that pulse-quickening moment when they get tickets
to a gig at Village Underground. Why? Well, music venues don't get
cooler. This place is strong on atmosphere, thanks to its industrial
warehouse vibe. Apparently 1,000 people can fit in here but it never
feels that way – there's always a sense of intimacy despite its size.

THE 100 CLUB

Map 1; Century House, 100 Oxford Street, Fitzrovia;
///wisdom.basis.spared; www.the100club.co.uk

Look for the red sign above a nondescript door to find the legendary
100 Club. Inside, descend the venue's stairs and you'll discover decor
that's not changed since the 70s, a little stage that's welcomed the likes
of The Rolling Stones and music lovers bopping along with live bands.

Shh!

Shoreditch's Troy Bar *(www.
troybar.co.uk)* bills itself as
London's best-kept secret. One
night spent swaying along to
live funk jams or reggae acts
– stopping only to tuck into
house-made Caribbean fare –
or daring to participate in
Tuesdays' open mic nights
will leave you with a serious
dilemma: to shout it from the
rooftops, or keep the secret to
yourself? Either way, you'll be
making a return visit.

Culture Live

Sure, the West End has its place but the real drama is found in the city's indie theatres and performance spaces. Dance, drag, burlesque, comedy – whatever you're into, London's got it.

WILTON'S MUSIC HALL

Map 2; 1 Graces Alley, Whitechapel; ///bottom.prompting.fish; www.wiltons.org.uk

Fancy a night of swinging mischief with an all-female cabaret band? Or one-man show "The One With Gunther", which retells the entirety of *Friends* in an hour? Join a kooky crowd and immerse yourself in fringe theatre at Wilton's, the world's oldest surviving music hall.

» Don't leave without having a drink at the Mahogony Bar, which was built back in 1826 and was later used as a soup kitchen during the Blitz.

BARBICAN CENTRE

Map 2; Silk Street, Barbican; ///forces.rubble.lake; www.barbican.org.uk

Don't be fooled by the stark 1980s exterior; the Barbican is a cultural powerhouse. Home of the London Symphony Orchestra and Royal Shakespeare Company, here you'll also discover curious art exhibitions, indie cinema screenings and electric live performances.

SADLER'S WELLS

Map 1; Rosebery Avenue, Angel; ///hints.square.tracks;
www.sadlerswells.com

Dance lovers know there's no beating Sadler's Wells, London's
dedicated home for contemporary dance with over three centuries'
worth of theatrical heritage. A stripped-back, unfussy space, here you'll
find an accessible programme of dance in all forms: loosened-up
ballet, Bollywood, fiery flamenco, street dance and bags more besides.

THE BILL MURRAY

Map 2; 39 Queens Head Street, Angel; ///quiz.feeds.rash;
www.angelcomedy.co.uk

There's no mistaking which London pub is dedicated to comedy: the
mural of Charlie Chaplin is a giveaway. Once a shabby pub, the Bill
Murray was taken over by Angel Comedy Club, which also hosts
stand-up nights at the Camden Head down the road. There's a free
show every night, so it's always busy with Londoners looking for a
laugh. Cross your fingers for a celeb comic trying out new material.

Try it!
STAND-UP COMEDY

Got a notebook filled with jokes that you've
been waiting to try on an audience? Email
raw@angelcomedy.co.uk as far in advance
as you can and test your mettle on one of
the most welcoming comedy stages in town.

Solo, Pair, Crowd

A day to yourself? Struggling for date night ideas? Craving a night out with the gang? London's cultural scene has got something for every occasion.

FLYING SOLO

Perfect your poetry

Always fancied performing at a spoken word gig? The Southbank Centre runs a monthly Out-Spoken Masterclass, where you can hone your work with the guidance of an experienced poet.

IN A PAIR

Cuddle up at an intimate gig

Founded in a London living room, Sofar Sounds now hosts gigs with unknowns in unusual places across the city. You might get a jazz band, a spoken-word artist or a classical flautist. Just bring beer and blankets.

FOR A CROWD

Watch musical legends with the crew

Get tickets for a gig at Camden's glorious Roundhouse (p140). You can't beat the feeling of rocking out with all your pals around you.

THE OLD VIC

Map 5; The Cut, Waterloo; ///scores.master.grid;
www.oldvictheatre.com

Ah, the Old Vic. The world-leading, not-for-profit theatre has staged more national treasures than any other since it opened in 1818. And it's yours for a snip. Preview tickets go on sale five weeks in advance, and are just £10. Keep an eye on the website for release dates.

SOUTHBANK CENTRE

Map 5; Belvedere Road, South Bank; ///alien.cave.discouraged;
www.southbankcentre.co.uk

A vast, Brutalist concrete slab on the banks of the Thames, the Southbank Centre is loved by Londoners. The backdrop for after-work drinks, it also happens to be one of the city's best cultural hubs with its three venues showcasing gigs, theatre, debates and more.

BETHNAL GREEN WORKING MEN'S CLUB

Map 2; 42–4 Pollard Row, Bethnal Green; ///angle.epic.elaborate;
www.workersplaytime.net

Mischief is key to a night at this former working men's club, which has been hosting socials since 1887. Bring your entourage and get ready to slay with a glorious cast of alternative queens and performers. It's about as inclusive, quirky and raucous as an East London night can be.

» Don't leave without heading downstairs to the cosy Workers Arms for a quick pint and game of Jenga with a more sedate crowd.

Cool Clubs

*Clubbing in London is a world-class experience.
Top-tier DJs keep movers and shakers dancing every
night of the week, with line-ups easily competing
with some of the world's most famous superclubs.*

PECKHAM AUDIO

Map 5; 133A Rye Lane, Peckham; ///lifts.curving.rice;
www.peckhamaudio.co.uk

After a hard week at work, the city's coolest chuck on their favourite
trainers and make for a night out in Peckham. Some of South London's
best nightlife outfits are found along Rye Lane, not least subterranean
Peckham Audio. This exclusive venue has quietly made a name for
itself on the alternative clubbing circuit thanks to its top-of-the-range
sound system and top-notch house and techno producers.

XOYO

Map 2; 32–7 Cowper Street, Shoreditch; ///quest.bath.soup;
www.xoyo.co.uk

It's no exaggeration to say that London's best electronic line-ups are
found at this underground Shoreditch staple. XOYO's programme
favours quality music and genres span house, techno, drum and

bass, grime and hip hop. DJ residencies are world-class – Palms Trax, Andy C, Calibre to name a few – and keep London's party people dancing into the early hours of the morning.

>> **Don't leave without** swinging by the Banksy graffiti, hidden behind a kebab shop around the corner (where Old Street meets Great Eastern).

GREMIO DE BRIXTON

Map 5; St Matthews Church, Brixton Hill, Brixton; ///pills.sugar.closet; www.gremiodebrixton.com

Gremio's setting, in a candle-lit tapas bar beneath a church, may sound more like date territory than big night out, but don't be fooled – this place is less than holy. Come late evening, couples slink home after a romantic dinner and the candles are extinguished as South London's 20-somethings take over the crypt. Catch them shooting shots at the bar, fist-pumping to old-school hits and belting out ABBA bangers.

FOLD

Map 6; Gillian House, Canning Town; ///flight.passes.state; www.fold.london

This 600-capacity ravers' dream opened its doors in 2018 with a hedonistic electro programme. Its industrial setting is in the middle of nowhere (though rest assured there's a Tube station within a 10-minute walk) so party nights feel private, further helped by the strict photography ban on the dance floor. Be ready to let loose and dance with abandon alongside clubbers whose spirits hark back to the 1990s warehouse days.

TOOTING TRAM & SOCIAL

Map 6; 46–8 Mitcham Road, Tooting; ///intend.churn.types;
www.tootingtramandsocial.co.uk

It may not look much from the outside but this cavernous converted tram shed promises a great night. A casual hangout in the day, come evening the table football and time-worn chesterfield sofas are pushed aside as a fun and friendly crowd of young professionals dance to hip hop and R'n'B classics.

BRIXTON JAMM

Map 5; 261 Brixton Road, Brixton; ///spots.stow.pest;
www.brixtonjamm.org

Brixton Jamm is a shapeshifter. A favoured student haunt and the site of many community-focused events, the versatile venue is also a favoured after-party spot for O2 Academy gig-goers. Here you'll

Shh!

Sign up for emails from Keep Hush *(www.keephush.net)*, an ultra-secret underground dance-music event that hosts DJ nights across London. You'll get announcements with dates before receiving word of the event's location on the day itself.

Even the lineup is a secret – one day you'll find yourself at a grime night, the next at a house-music rave. Prefer to party with your pals at home? Keep Hush also runs weekly live music streams, so you can party in the comfort of your front room.

find disco day parties on its huge terrace, sweaty grime sessions in its (thankfully air-conditioned) main room and actor and DJ Craig Charles's legendary Funk and Soul Club.

RIDLEY ROAD MARKET BAR
**Map 3; 49 Ridley Road, Dalston; ///item.forgot.farm;
www.ridleyroadmarketbar.com**

This scruffbag spot masks its office-like panelled ceilings and sticky floors with tropical décor in its bid for a tiki beach bar vibe. The drinks are cheap, with tins of Red Stripe at £4.50 cocktails £7. And the beats of Motown and reggae keeps a down-to-earth crowd dancing until the lights are turned up in the early hours. Leave your pretentions at the door (and start queuing for the toilet 15 minutes in advance).
» Don't leave without enjoying a 10-inch, £5 pizza from Slice Girls, self-named "90s babes" who have been feeding partygoers since 2013.

DALSTON SUPERSTORE
**Map 3; 117 Kingsland High Street, Dalston; ///remove.brief.heads;
www.dalstonsuperstore.com**

Indie LGBTQ+ venues are under threat in London, falling victim to the city's rising rents and property development. This fact makes the community vibe and consistently full dance floor at Superstore feel even more special. Londoners flock here for the club's fondness for drag queens dancing on the bar, the queer art displayed all over the walls, and the club's wonderful ability to segue from sickly sweet pop upstairs to dark, techno filth in the basement.

LGBTQ+ Scene

London is globally recognized as an LGBTQ+ capital, thanks to its vibrant queer history and fabulous nightlife scene. You'll be welcomed with open arms at a number of inclusive venues and theatre spots.

THE GLORY

Map 2; 281 Kingsland Road, Haggerston; ///stale.pill.cared; www.theglory.co

Drag queen superstar Jonny Woo teamed up with drag DJ John Sizzle to launch this performance powerhouse and party pub. It's become big on the scene since its 2015 opening, thanks to its glittering stage hosting a whole lotta drag. In daylight hours, The Glory holds talks about the history of gay life in Hackney; come nightfall, things get steamy in the basement, when a young, alternative crowd hit the floor.

ROYAL VAUXHALL TAVERN

Map 5; 372 Kennington Lane, Vauxhall; ///master.plank.stable; www.vauxhalltavern.com

It's said that after a nuclear holocaust all that would be left are cockroaches, Cher and the Royal Vauxhall Tavern. This legendary Grade II-listed performance venue dates back to 1863 but it left its Victorian sensibilities behind many moons ago. The RVT has played a key role in London's and, more specifically, Vauxhall's gay history. And the community love it, so much so that they've campaigned to protect the tavern from property developers countless times. No trip to central London is complete without popping into this sacred place.

» **Don't leave without** upping the ante at Fire, just around the corner. It's a great way to complete your experience of gay nightlife in Vauxhall.

ABOVE THE STAG THEATRE

Map 5; 72 Albert Embankment, Vauxhall; ///menu.loudly.rises; www.abovethestag.org.uk

Above the Stag is the UK's only full-time, professional LGBTQ+ theatre company. It has one fundamental aim: to use storytelling to give an elevated voice to the community. To that end, musicals, plays, readings, comedy and more all have their turn in the limelight here. Come December, the theatre hosts the one Christmas pantomime it's definitely worth donning your festive knit for. The company is currently looking for a new place of residence, so keep your eyes peeled on the website for more information.

SHE SOHO

Map 1; 23A Old Compton Street, Soho; ///scales.racing.thing; www.ku-bar.co.uk

London's only exclusively queer women's venue is all about having a good time with lively DJ sets and top-drawer drag king peformances. Though mainly catering to women, everyone is welcome; the organizers just want people to party hard in a safe space.

Liked by the locals

"As a queer person, London has always felt like home. Its rich history of Queerness is reflected in its proliferation of LGBTQ+ venues and spaces; here there's a unique combination of anonymity and acceptance, which creates a freedom to exist as you are."

MAX SLACK, LGBTQ+ INFLUENCER, CONSULTANT, CONTENT CREATOR AND SPEAKER

ADONIS AT E1

Map 2; Unit 2, 110 Pennington Street, Wapping; ///snack.those.wasp; https://adonis.eventcube.io

Nights out don't get more in-your-face than Adonis. Expect risqué outfits, delicious debauchery and thumping techno as a mob of young ravers live their best lives. The queer underground event really does foster a feeling of inclusivity.

BIG DYKE ENERGY

Map 5; Unit 18, Surrey Canal Road, Bermondsey; ///quiz.boost.events; www.bigdykeenergyldn.co.uk

The clue is in the name: this place is all about the empowerment of queer women. Anything goes in this no-rules club: dress up or dress down. Hit the floor with no inhibitions or stick to the bar. Bring your friends or come alone. No matter what, you'll feel the joy of the party.

THE KARAOKE HOLE

Map 3; 95 Kingsland High Street, Dalston; ///breath.drive.haven; www.thekaraokehole.com

The owners of Dalston Superstore have blessed Londoners with a genius concept: karaoke led by the city's finest drag stars. At Karaoke Hole, expect a fabulous host to encourage and mock you through your rendition of "Like a Virgin". Want more? Just wait for the arrival of Geri Halliwell impersonator Just May, or the inspiring Mahatma Khandi.

» Don't leave without grabbing an enormous slice of pizza from Voodoo Ray's, upstairs from the Karaoke Hole.

SHACKLEWELL LANE

1 **A bite to eat at**
DEL74
Chow down on tacos and quesadillas while bopping to retro tunes at this jolly haunt.

The indie **Rio Cinema** *has been screening films since 1915 but, in the 70s, it briefly staged live burlesque and striptease acts.*

KINGSLAND HIGH ST

SANDRINGHAM ROAD

Grab the mic at
THE KARAOKE HOLE
2
A cohort of drag queens host nights at this underground spot. Prepare your best Madonna impersonation for a karaoke experience like no other.

Ridley Road *might be quiet at night but during the day it's a busy marketplace – a scene that's little changed since the 1980s.*

BRADBURY STREET

KINGSLAND HIGH STREET

BOLEYN ROAD

DALSTON

RIDLEY ROAD

3 **A quick game at**
DRAUGHTS
Need a breather? Head to this low-key board game bar for a glass of wine and game of Jenga or Hungry Hippos.

0 metres   100
0 yards   100

An evening in
Dalston's dive bars

The secret's out: Dalston is where it's at. People flock here from all over town (and farther afield) to be seen in the neighbourhood's basement bars, vegan restaurants and backstreet pubs. Rising rents have seen the end of some beloved grassroots nightlife spots, but Dalston is still one of London's most vibrant and multicultural areas. You can't get to know East London without spending a night trawling Kingsland High Street, ideally after an afternoon shopping in its indie boutiques and charity shops.

1. Del74
129 Kingsland High Street, Dalston;
www.tacosdel74.com;
///guards.finely.update

2. The Karaoke Hole
95 Kingsland High Street, Dalston;
www.thekaraokehole.com;
///truck.cool.tens

3. Draughts
41 Kingsland High Street, Dalston;
www.draughtslondon.com;
///privately.occurs.tubes

4. Ridley Road Market Bar
49 Ridley Road, Dalston;
www.ridleyroadmarket bar.com;
///item.forgot.farm

Rio Cinema ///dimes. copies.during

COLVESTONE CRESCENT

4
Dance at
RIDLEY ROAD
MARKET BAR
End the night's proceedings at this tropical-themed locals' spot, where the beers are cheap and the tunes are banging.

OUTDOORS

It might be a metropolis but London isn't lacking on the outdoors front. Come rain or shine, locals love nothing more than a walk in the park or a dip in an open-air lido.

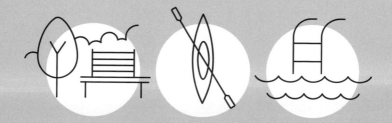

Swimming Spots

As far as a Londoner is concerned, anything above 24°C is summer. With sunglasses on and swimmers at the ready, it's straight to a lido, where it's as much about being seen as it is actually swimming.

SERPENTINE LIDO

Map 4; Hyde Park, Kensington; ///starts.buzz.popped;
www.royalparks.org.uk

Come summer and Hyde Park's resident swans are forced to share this lido with the masses. Sun-worshippers pepper the grounds around the water, rowers glide just beyond the swimming barrier and mates enjoy a splash around. Things are quieter for the swans in winter, though the hardy members of the Serpentine Swimming Club – Britain's oldest of its kind –continue to plunge into the chilly depths each morning.

LONDON FIELDS LIDO

Map 3; London Fields West Side, Hackney; ///unit.learns.river;
www.better.org.uk

You'll be pleased to hear that London Fields' Olympic-sized pool is heated so whatever the weather you're in for a pleasant dip. And you'll really enjoy the buzzy community vibes, too. Young Hackney parents dip their babies in the water here and friends compete over who can swim the most lengths, before hardcore swimmers arrive for a peaceful evening swim beneath the lido's flapping bunting.

>> Don't leave without a pick-me-up coffee and falafel wrap from the café. Enjoy on the terrace while watching your fellow swimmers.

BROCKWELL LIDO

Map 5; Brockwell Park, Dulwich Road, Brixton; ///petal.broom.open; www.brockwelllido.com

Set on the fringes of Brockwell Park, this outdoor pool is a beloved landmark – so much so that you can even get married here. The Grade II-listed Art Deco building that surrounds the waters makes for an attractive backdrop (it also houses the popular Lido Café, which does a knockout brunch). The pool is unheated so it's one for the hardcore swimmers among you – though when a heatwave hits, the lido is suddenly at the forefront of everyone's minds.

CHARLTON LIDO

Map 6; Hornfair Park, Shooters Hill Road, Greenwich; ///haven.curvy.chin; www.better.org.uk

Charlton Lido's claims to fame include starring in a Blazin' Squad music video in 2003 and an episode of police drama *The Bill* in 2004. Such dizzying heights aside, the 1930s lido underwent a £2 million facelift in 2013 and now it has it all: two sun terraces, a gym, and a state-of-the-art fitness studio, plus a fully heated pool. Bring your own squad and enjoy a dip; it's open all year round.

HAMPSTEAD HEATH PONDS

Map 6; Hampstead Heath, Hampstead; ///jobs.crown.ranged;
www.hampsteadheath.net

A community of thick-skinned regulars swim here through the winter.
For mere mortals, it's the first signs of summer that put the heath's
Mixed Pond and its segregated alternatives on the map. Yes, the
waters are murky and ducks bob about on the surface, but going
wild swimming here is the best escape from the city.

PARLIAMENT HILL LIDO

Map 6; Heath Lodge, Highgate; ///money.added.goes;
www.parliamenthilllido.org

Don't fancy sharing your swim with the local wildlife of Hampstead?
Then head to the heath's other dipping option, the Parliament Hill
Lido. Dating way back to 1934, it's always a few degrees warmer
and altogether more refined than its neighbour.

» Don't leave without making use of the lido's toasty sauna, perfect
for drying off after a bracing dip.

TOOTING BEC LIDO

Map 6; Tooting Bec Road, Tooting; ///case.badge.raced; www.slsc.org.uk

This is the largest outdoor freshwater pool in the UK and arguably
London's most popular lido. When school's out for summer, excited
kids and their weary parents head to Tooting Bec Lido to splash about
in its waters. Meanwhile groups of friends line the concrete to chat,
people-watch and top up their vitamin D before taking a cooling dip.

Liked by the locals

"The ponds don't feel like London. I love going first thing, when it's freezing and misty. Everyone's bonded by the cold – shivering but smiling. And you can tell who the hardcore swimmers are by their sensible woolly hats."

NESS WHEELER, YOGA TEACHER, FILM PRODUCER AND REGULAR SWIMMER AT HAMPSTEAD HEATH LADIES' POND

Green Spaces

This is the world's first National Park City, didn't you know? Londoners are very proud of this fact, and rightly so. After all, there are countless parks, rich with wildlife, sitting right on their doorstep.

RICHMOND PARK

Map 6; entrance via Richmond Gate, Richmond; ///barks.vine.fees; www.royalparks.org.uk

Some Londoners might say that Richmond isn't *really* in London, it being so far out, but that would be denying the city its greatest slice of wilderness. A rambling expanse of tousled meadows, dappled woodland and reed-fringed ponds, this is where city-dwellers go to let off steam and get closer to nature. Things are quieter on weekdays,

Try it!
PHOTOGRAPH NATURE

Extend your time in leafy Richmond with a trip to Kew Gardens, a botanical masterpiece. Here you can join photography classes with specialist tree and forest photographer Edward Parker.

when roaming herds of deer rule the park, but come the weekend it's a hive of activity – dog-walkers stop to make conversation, cyclists tackle the muddy tracks and groups walk off their Sunday roasts.

HAMPSTEAD HEATH

Map 6; entrance via South End Road, Hampstead; ///fakes.prime.album; www.hampsteadheath.net

Just a couple of stops on the underground from gritty Camden is Hampstead Heath, the wild, undulating lungs of North London. You could spend days rambling across the heath's acres of parkland and foraging in its fruitful meadows, not forgetting dipping a toe in one of its willowy ponds *(p162)*. However long you're here, a walk up to Parliament Hill for its spectacular views of the London skyline is essential, especially followed by a pint at the Spaniards Inn *(p72)*.

» Don't leave without wandering through the plant-entangled Hampstead Hill Gardens and Pergola – it's elegant and eerie all at once.

VICTORIA PARK

Map 3; entrance via Crown Gate East, Bow; ///poppy.hears.deny

Families hot-foot it to the boating lake, friends play rounders on the lawn, joggers thud along the running track; this green space lives up to its moniker of the "People's Park", so given in Victorian times because it was intended for the use of ordinary East Enders. In the summer, when festivals aren't on, Vicky Park (another affectionate nickname) is the place to come armed with a bottle of plonk and fresh supplies from nearby Victoria Park Village's delis and bakeries.

LONDON FIELDS

Map 3; entrance on Lansdowne Drive, Hackney; ///clever.zips.fills

There's a lovely village feel about London Fields, thanks in part to its proximity to independent-led Broadway Market *(p100)*. Grandads read the paper on park benches, looking up to watch families cycling along the park's paths. Hipsters sprawled across the grass, coffees in hand, put the world to rights. Competitive couples battle it out at the communal ping pong table. This is the place to while away a Saturday.

BROCKWELL PARK

Map 5; entrance via Brixton Water Lane, Brixton; ///carry.latter.object

Plonked between the hubbubs of Brixton, Herne Hill and Tulse Hill, Brockwell Park is a much, much-needed slice of greenery. Something is always afoot in the vast expanse of green, whether it's a Saturday Park Run, a basketball tournament or an alfresco birthday party. Come July, the Lambeth Country Show moves in for a weekend of animal displays, music performances and vegetable-growing competitions.

» Don't leave without visiting the hidden garden at Brockwell's western edge – it's a walled-off oasis with lots of quiet benches.

PRIMROSE HILL

Map 6; entrance via Primrose Hill Road, Primrose Hill; ///hook.sand.keys

A hot contender for London's loveliest picnic spot, Primrose Hill rises up above the gastropubs, delis and cafés of Regent's Park Road, offering a cracking view of the city. In summer, its gentle incline is dotted with sunbathers and gaggles of friends; in autumn, locals huddle on the

Sunrise is the best time to admire the view from atop Primrose Hill —and you'll have it all to yourself.

slope to watch fireworks blaze across the skyline on Guy Fawkes night. And when winter sees snow, makeshift sledges miraculously appear overnight.

CRYSTAL PALACE PARK

Map 6; entrance via Thicket Road, Crystal Palace; ///model.tried.fade; www.crystalpalacepark.org.uk

Crystal Palace residents will proudly point out that this isn't your average patch of grass. For one, this former Victorian Pleasure Ground survived the fire that destroyed the eponymous Crystal Palace. What they really love to talk about, though, are the dinosaurs. Strangely lumpy, quirky remnants of Victoriana, these concrete sculptures were the world's first life-size dinosaur replicas and have become beloved mascots of this area. If you're more about puzzles than prehistoric creatures, there's a maze that dates back to 1870.

Covent Garden can be a bit much, with bag-laden shoppers and excitable theatre-goers. Thankfully, the garden of the Actors' Church is on hand *(www.actorschurch.org)*. Enter through the iron gates on

Bedford Street, at the back of Covent Garden, and you'll find lush green lawns flanking the path, which is also lined with benches and strings of fairy lights. Peaceful and pretty, it's the perfect spot for some down time.

On the Water

For all its concrete and brick, London is a city shaped around water – river buses shuttle commuters along the Thames, rowing boats criss-cross the Serpentine and walkers stomp alongside willowy canals.

PADDLEBOARD ON REGENT'S CANAL

Map 1; start at the Pirate Castle, Oval Road, Camden; ///people.weds.bets

Okay, SUPing might seem better paired with the golden beaches of California than Britain's concrete capital. But paddleboarding has caught on here too and Regent's Canal is the place to do it. The stretch between Camden and Little Venice is particularly picturesque. Work your core as you paddle past the residents of London Zoo and river dwellers tending to their canal boat roof gardens.

SIGHTSEE ABOARD THE THAMES CLIPPER

Map 4; start at Putney Pier; ///gladiators.cure.cubs; www.thamesclippers.com

The glorious vistas, on-board coffee and guaranteed seats of the commuter-friendly Thames Clippers are a far cry from the cramped confines of rush hour on the Tube. It's a great way to travel: the river

After some culture? Hop on the Clipper for the half-hour ride between Tate Britain and the Tate Modern. bus zips between 23 piers, giving you a front-row view of countless London landmarks. Make a day of it by starting in Putney and disembarking in Greenwich.

FOLLOW THE WANDLE TRAIL

Map 6; start at Carshalton Ponds, Carshalton; ///summer.scared.work; www.wandlevalleypark.co.uk

A lot of Londoners haven't even heard of the River Wandle, which snakes through South London. Cyclists who have, however, spend their Saturdays following this 14-km (9-mile) route as it meanders through a clutch of parks that line the watercourse. Begin at Carshalton Ponds or, if you just fancy a taster, pick it up at Wimbledon Park.

» Don't leave without sinking a frothy pint at appropriately named pub The Wandle, just by Earlsfield train station.

WALK THE THAMES PATH

Map 4; start from Putney Pier; ///drift.glee.quit; www.thames-path.org.uk

The River Thames is the very heart of London and every local has enjoyed a long walk along the Thames Path – it's the perfect way to blow away the cobwebs. Start in Putney, where rowing clubhouses line the riverbanks, and stroll towards Teddington, then follow the gravelly track that winds along the water's edge all the way to elegant Richmond. Tuck into a slap-up dinner at one of the gastropubs here before jumping on a train back to the city.

Solo, Pair, Crowd

Whether you're travelling alone, in a duo or en masse, there's a watery adventure to fit every gathering.

FLYING SOLO
Water and wheels
See the city from two wheels by hiring a bike and cycling along the Regent's Canal towpath. Begin east in Victoria Park and pedal west, concluding in charming Little Venice, where you can enjoy a congratulatory waterside drink.

IN A PAIR
A boat for two on the Serpentine
Grab your best mate, or a family member, and a few provisions and take a rowing boat or pedalo across the serene waters of the Serpentine in Hyde Park.

FOR A CROWD
Party on a boat
Bring a blowout picnic and all your squad to board the beautiful *Jenny Wren* as it navigates Regent's Canal (*www.walkersquay.com*).

WALTHAMSTOW WETLANDS

**Map 6; 2 Forest Road, Walthamstow; ///combining.share.food;
www.walthamstowwetlands.com;**

The long-standing domain of rare wildfowl, Europe's largest urban wetlands were opened to the public in 2017. Today the reservoirs don't just attract anglers and birders. Couples stroll hand in hand along the boardwalks, families enjoy leisurely picnics and mates cycle along the paths en route to Walthamstow's craft breweries.

» Don't leave without checking out the Wetlands Contemporary art programme at the Engine House, by the wetlands' entrance.

WATERBUS RIDES TO CAMDEN

**Map 4; start at Warwick Crescent, Little Venice; ///pulse.onion.envy;
www.londonwaterbus.com**

Looking for date inspiration? This cutesy canalboat trundles up and down arguably the prettiest part of Regent's Canal. Embark at Little Venice and chug along to buzzy Camden Lock. Jump off here before tucking into snacks at eco-focused Buck Street Market.

MUDLARKING ON THE NORTH BANK

**Map 2; access via the Trig Lane Stairs, North Bank; ///seats.sizes.clear;
www.thames-explorer.org.uk**

The tidal waters of the Thames churn up remnants of the past, with low tide unveiling time-lost detritus. Join a guide (safety first, remember) and a friendly community of mudlarkers to beachcomb for lost treasures; it will give you new insight into the city.

Cemetery Strolls

We know, it sounds odd, but London's gorgeous cemetery grounds – especially the so-called "Magnificent Seven" – are ideal for an afternoon's ramble or a simple bit of R & R.

ABNEY PARK CEMETERY

Map 3; 215 Stoke Newington High Street, Stoke Newington; ///sung.animal.bigger; www.abneypark.org

Wild and woody Abney Park Cemetery, perhaps most famous for featuring in the music video for Amy Winehouse's "Back to Black", is a great place to walk off brunch in the company of Stokey's past residents. Look for the graves of rebels, panto actors and a chap who taught the Victorians all about African and Asian wildlife – essentially the 19th-century David Attenborough (the lion on his grave is the clue).

HIGHGATE CEMETERY

Map 6; Swain's Lane, Highgate; ///audio.regard.scrap; www.highgatecemetery.org

It's hard to resist the grand allure of Highgate, with its towering monuments and statues. This is the final resting place of some big names; Karl Marx, George Eliot and Douglas Adams are all buried here, plus Alexander Litvinenko, who is buried in a lead coffin to prevent radioactive leaking. Join an organized tour on a Wednesday to learn more about other residents and how the Victorians were generally obsessed with death, which explains why London has all of these epic cemeteries littered with elaborate crypts.

» Don't leave without paying your respects at the grave of suffragist Ernestine Rose, who is dubbed the first Jewish feminist.

KENSAL GREEN CEMETERY

Map 4; Harrow Road, Kensal Green; ///rooms.insist.tight;
www.kensalgreencemetery.com

One of the oldest of the Magnificent Seven, Kensal Green Cemetery certainly has a Gothic noire quality about it. Horror films have been shot here and, in real life, the grounds have experienced some weird goings-on, including one poor pallbearer being killed by a coffin he was carrying. All this aside, the cemetery is an area of conservation and home to more than 30 species of bird, who break the eerie silence with their cheerful song.

BUNHILL FIELDS BURIAL GROUND

Map 2; 38 City Road, Old Street; ///gained.second.hurry; 020 7374 4127

Grab a latte at nearby Workshop Coffee and take a turn around Bunhill Fields. It's not one of London's most famous, but it's easy to see why city slickers choose to eat their lunch in the company of Daniel Defoe and William Blake. This square of calming green offers genuine respite from the frenetic pace of central London.

WANDSWORTH CEMETERY

Map 6; 32 Magdalen Road, Wandsworth; ///wiping.remark.limes; www.wandsworth.gov.uk

Okay, it's not as grand as other London cemeteries, so why visit Wandsworth Cemetery? Aside from the pretty and perfectly manicured grounds, the cemetery's views out over South London are hard to beat. And while an onslaught of joggers, families and raucous 20-somethings descend on nearby Wandsworth Common, you'll have the cemetery all to yourself.

NUNHEAD CEMETERY

Map 5; Linden Grove, Nunhead; ///slim.forest.preoccupied; www.fonc.org.uk

This is the biggest of the Magnificent Seven and it's also the grandest. Tree-lined walkways sweep around its grounds, which are punctuated with huge tombs, monuments and the beautiful ruins of

Shh!

Many don't realize that down the road from Mile End Park and Victoria Park is Tower Hamlets Cemetery. You might mistake it for a spit of woodland, being as wild and unkept as it is; graves vie for space with flora and fauna and tree roots break up headstones. The East End was historically the city's poorest quarter and this is the graveyard of its ordinary people – around 350,000 residents in total. Wander the winding paths and, if you're not squeamish, forage the fertile ground for wild garlic.

an Anglican chapel. Speaking of grandeur, on the cemetery's western side you'll get a wonderful vista including St Paul's Cathedral and, on a clear day, beloved venue Alexandra Palace on the horizon. The groundsmen are even considerate enough to trim the trees to allow for an uninterrupted view.

BROCKLEY CEMETERY

Map 5; Ivy Road, Deptford; ///shot.manage.spits; www.foblc.org.uk

As mentioned, the Victorians loved the macabre so they were naturally fascinated by Brockley Cemetery, where poisoner Amelia Winters was buried not far from murdered teen Jane Maria Clouson. Grim, but the grounds remain a pleasant place for a walk followed by a cheering drink at Brockley Brewery just down the road.

>> Don't leave without visiting the adjacent Ladywell Cemetery, which opened within a month of its sister.

BROMPTON CEMETERY

Map 4; Fulham Road, Kensington; ///labs.lively.castle;
www.brompton-cemetery.org.uk

Locals call Brompton the Cemetery of Light and Sun because both the inventors of sunglasses and traffic lights are buried here. And a walk here is especially lovely on a mellow summer or autumn day, when a golden light is cast across the grounds. Search for the grave of suffragette Emmeline Pankhurst and socialite Hannah Courtoy's tomb (which the Victorians believed was a time machine – weird) before concluding with a coffee in the cemetery's Café North Lodge.

Community Gardens and Urban Farms

Volunteer-led gardens and urban farms are a little-known side to London. Escape the heaving metropolis and get your hands dirty with the locals at one of these little rural outposts.

THE STORY GARDEN

Map 1; Ossulston Street, Kings Cross; ///salon.down.lonely; www.globalgeneration.org.uk

This community garden, grown in upcycled skips, has transformed a plot of land behind the Barbican Library. The Story Garden is a sustainable urban oasis built by and for the locals; a place to grow herbs and veg, and escape the furore of the city.

PHYTOLOGY MEDICINAL GARDEN

Map 2; Bethnal Green Nature Reserve, Middleton Street, Bethnal Green; ///usage.glue.codes; www.phytology.org.uk

Puffs of yellow dandelions, dense clumps of nettles and dainty chamomile are grown in abundance on this transformed World War II bombsite. Set amid the woodland of Bethnal Green Nature

Reserve, this apothecary garden celebrates the medicinal power of the humble weed. And the community vibes are palpable. Stop by and an expert gardener in overalls will diagnose your latest ailment and point you in the direction of the plant to pick.

SURREY DOCKS FARM

Map 5; Rotherhithe Street, Surrey Quays; ///silly.walks.handy; www.surreydocksfarm.org.uk

While stressed bankers in suits pound the floors of Canary Wharf's skyscrapers, a blacksmith in old-fashioned garb hammers red-hot slabs of metal on Surrey Docks Farm. This farm is incongruous but it's a welcome slice of rural life. Local schoolkids learn about the city's farming history, creatives partake in ceramic classes and couples stock up on seasonal veg in the farm shop.

VAUXHALL CITY FARM

Map 5; 165 Tyers Street, Vauxhall; ///pram.entertainer.woes; www.vauxhallcityfarm.org

An afternoon spent on this central city farm might involve sheep-shearing demos or a chance to feed the chickens. But donate even just a couple of pounds on arrival and know that your visit means much more besides. The folk here are passionate about supporting young people in the community with outreach and development programmes, reaching 7,000 local school children every year.

» Don't leave without popping into the nearby Tea House Theatre, which serves refreshing loose-leaf teas and slabs of homemade cake.

DALSTON EASTERN CURVE GARDEN

Map 3; Dalston Lane, Hackney; ///hobby.ladder.wiped;
www.dalstongarden.org

A social enterprise since 2012, Dalston's eco garden – built on an old railway track – is an oasis. Bees drift from herb to flower and groups of friends catch up on tree stumps in the fairy-lit garden, usually to the soundtrack of someone strumming a guitar.

HACKNEY CITY FARM

Map 2; 1A Goldsmiths Row, Hackney; ///global.spin.flag;
www.hackneycityfarm.co.uk

Almost entirely run by volunteers, Hackney City Farm is all about community. Green-fingered locals pitch in with the garden, 30-somethings in hand-knitted jumpers pick up produce and kids make friends with the animals. Come for weekend brunch at its café and you'll be offering to harvest some veg before you know it.
» Don't leave without buying a pot of their home-produced honey. It's so good that you're only allowed two jars per person.

CULPEPER COMMUNITY GARDEN

Map 1; 1 Cloudesley Road, Angel; ///foster.chops.custom;
www.culpeper.org.uk

Local volunteers from all backgrounds tend to this wonderful garden, hidden by high walls, and each puts their own personal stamp on the flowery scene. They'll most likely be pouring a cuppa in the tea hut as you arrive; join them before a tour.

Liked by the locals

"Both nature and people flourish in community gardens. They are London's mini havens, where we can connect with others and with the earth; there's nothing more satisfying than having a cup of freshly picked mint tea after working together in the garden."

ABI JOHNSTON, CLINICAL SCIENTIST AND BROCKWELL PARK COMMUNITY GARDEN VOLUNTEER

Nearby Getaways

Of course Londoners love their city but sometimes a change of scene and gulp of fresh air are just what the doctor ordered. Luckily the capital has various tempting day trips in easy reach.

EPPING FOREST

1-hour Tube from Oxford Circus

Wedged between London and the county of Essex, this ancient woodland feels worlds away from the hubbub of the Big Smoke. So, come the weekend, those craving the great outdoors don their walking boots and set off on a hike along the sun-dappled forest floor, stopping to picnic by one of the ponds that punctuate the landscape and concluding their walk with a reviving pint in one of Epping's cosy pubs. Pure bliss.

BRIGHTON

1-hour train from Victoria station or 1.5 hour train from St Pancras International station; www.visitbrighton.com

Pebbly beaches dotted with optimistic sun-soakers, jaunty fairground rides and chirpy ice cream vans: for classic British seaside charms, Brighton ticks all the boxes. But many Londoners skip the beach entirely. After all, there are bargains to pick up in the Lanes' vintage shops, coffees to drink at independent roasters and a sustainably focused food scene to sample. All this in the most friendly and inclusive of communities. What more could you want?

>> Don't leave without renting a bike from one of the city's public docking stations and cycling along the seafront to nearby Hove, Brighton's chilled out next-door neighbour.

MARGATE

1.5-hour train from St Pancras International station; www.visitthanet.co.uk

Margate is the go-to coastal hotspot for hipster, arty types (hence the nickname Shoreditch-on-sea). Day-trippers come for a blast of salty-aired nostalgia, to browse the vintage shops and check out the Turner Contemporary. Margate may have experienced gentrification – there are craft beer, natural wine and independent coffee places galore – but it's kept its edge. Check out the retro rides at Dreamland for proof.

RYE

1-hour train from St Pancras International station

City slickers descend on Rye on their days off. And who can blame them? This hilltop town in East Sussex is pure charm, with its cobbled lanes, antique shops, wonky pubs and pretty harbour. Better still, the golden dunes of Camber Sands are a 5-km (3-mile) stroll away – perfect for walking off a slap-up meal of fish and chips. **» Don't leave without** ordering a scoop or two from Mermaid Street Café's ice cream window before walking up pretty Mermaid Street.

CAMBRIDGE

1.5-hour train from Kings Cross or Liverpool Street stations

Picture this: medieval streets thronging with students cycling to lectures, a river peppered with punting parties, crooked tea houses abuzz with chatter. Welcome to Cambridge, rival to the university city that-shall-not-be-named. This is the day trip Londoners roll out when they want to feel a bit more refined – a day out with the in-laws or a classy escape with the girls. Its magical charm never disappoints.

Try it!
GO PUNTING

Sure, you can pay someone to chauffeur you down the River Cam. But it's way more fun to impress your friends with your own punting skills. Book onto a lesson with a Scudamore's expert (*www.scudamores.com*).

THE CHILTERNS

30-minute train from Marylebone station or 1-hour Tube from Euston Square; www.visitchilterns.co.uk

Zip along on a train or Tube to the historic town of Amersham, the gateway to the beautiful Chilterns. Enjoy a riverside walk along the River Misbourne on arrival, pausing for lunch at one of the inviting pubs (perhaps The Swan, which has a lovely big garden and a great vegan menu). Then it's time for another dose of bracing fresh air with a country stroll in the surrounding Chiltern Hills. Lovely stuff.

BRISTOL

1.5-hour train from Paddington station; www.visitbristol.co.uk

If Londoners could live in another UK city, they would choose Bristol – this city is a hotbed for creativity, with cool start-ups popping up left, right and centre. And just think, if you did move, you could have all this: the street-art splashed streets of Stokes Croft, the view of ice-cream-hued houses teetering up the hills above the waterfront, the drama of the Clifton Suspension Bridge and the shipping container foodie hotspot of Wapping Wharf.

WHITSTABLE

1.5-hour train from Victoria or Cannon Street stations

Yes, this seaside town is a looker – boats bob out at sea, there are pastel-hued beach huts and atmospheric lanes – but it's the seafood that visitors have their eye on. A pint at the beachside Old Neptune is a must, as is getting oysters shucked right in front of you at The Forge.

0 metres 500
0 yards 500

HAMPSTEAD LANE

Stretch your legs on
HAMPSTEAD HEATH
Walk off your lunch in this
huge expanse of greenery.
If you're feeling brave, why not
take a dip in one of the ponds?

5

Tuck into lunch at
SPANIARDS INN
This charming pub is
always abuzz with families
and dog-walkers. Make
for the lovely, leafy beer
garden, which has plenty
of seats – the perfect
setting for a hearty roast.

4

SPANIARDS ROAD

MERTON LANE

HIGHGATE WEST HILL

Hampstead Heath

Mooch around
HAMPSTEAD VILLAGE
Wander through the cobbled
streets and stop to window-shop
at the antiques shops, fashion
boutiques and florists.

EAST HEATH RD

3

Enjoy the view from
PARLIAMENT HILL
VIEWPOINT
After climbing Parliament
Hill, take a breather and
drink in the incredible city
scenery from the summit.

2

HAMPSTEAD

1

HAMPSTEAD HIGH ST

DOWNSHIRE HILL

MANSFIELD ROAD

GOSPEL OAK

Grab coffee at
GINGER AND WHITE
Start with a flat white and slice
of carrot cake at one of the
pavement tables at this café,
tucked away in a pretty mews.

Romantic poet John
Keats lived at **Keats**
House *between 1818 and*
1820. Here he fell in love
with Fanny Brawne, who
lived opposite.

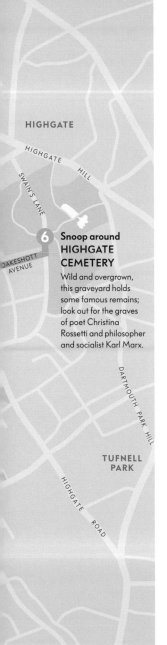

HIGHGATE

HIGHGATE HILL

SWAIN'S LANE

OAKESHOTT AVENUE

6 Snoop around
HIGHGATE CEMETERY
Wild and overgrown, this graveyard holds some famous remains; look out for the graves of poet Christina Rossetti and philosopher and socialist Karl Marx.

DARTMOUTH PARK HILL

TUFNELL PARK

HIGHGATE ROAD

A day in
idyllic Hampstead

Hampstead has it all: gorgeous mansions, trendy boutiques, characterful pubs and – the jewel in its crown – wild, undulating heathland. Long characterized by its intellectual, musical and literary residents, the north London neighbourhood is rich with history. Come the weekend, Londoners love nothing more than a stroll around the village and heath, fantasizing about their dream house and sighing over its picture-postcard scenery.

1. Ginger and White
4a–5a Perrin's Court;
www.gingerandwhite.com;
///tricky.dark.author

2. Hampstead Village
Hampstead High Street;
www.hampsteadvillage
london.com;
///cable.scuba.spicy

3. Parliament Hill Viewpoint
Hampstead Heath;
///tower.defeat.land

4. Spaniards Inn
Spaniards Road;
www.thespaniards
hampstead.co.uk;
///envy.logs.engine

5. Hampstead Heath
www.hampsteadheath.net;
///fakes.prime.album

6. Highgate Cemetery
Swain's Lane, Highgate;
www.highgatecemetery.org;
///audio.regard.scrap

📍 **Keats House** ///hangs.
booth.humans

With a little research and preparation, this city will feel like a home away from home. Check out these websites to ensure a healthy, safe stay in London.

London
DIRECTORY

SAFE SPACES

London is a wonderfully diverse and inclusive city, but should you feel uneasy or crave community at any point during your stay, there are spaces and resources to offer support.

www.blackownedlondon.com
A curated online guide to London's Black-owned businesses.

www.jw3.org.uk
An all-encompassing cultural centre for London's Jewish communities.

https://londonmandir.baps.org
A Hindu temple and welcoming cultural centre for all.

www.muslimsinbritain.org
The definitive guide to mosques and Muslim community spaces in the UK.

www.stonewall.org.uk
Charity offering support for the LGBTQ+ community, as well as a list of services and groups in your area.

www.switchboard.lgbt
An LGBTQ+ helpline to talk through any problems and find support among like-minded people.

HEALTH

The UK's National Health Service, the NHS, provides free emergency care for all, regardless of their nationality. Non-emergency care is usually not free, however, so make sure you take out comprehensive health insurance before you visit.

www.babylonhealth.com
Talk to a doctor or check your symptoms online via this NHS-affiliated service.

www.boots-uk.com
UK's leading pharmacy-led retailer with a Midnight Pharmacy service at 60 of its shops around London.

www.citizenaid.org
A resource full of first-aid tips.

www.guysandstthomas.nhs.uk
An A&E department and walk-in urgent care centre across the river from Big Ben.

www.homerton.nhs.uk/sexual-health
Walk-in sexual health clinic at Clifden Centre, Homerton University Hospital.

www.nhs.uk
The UK healthcare system's website, full of advice and a list of health centres.

TRAVEL SAFETY ADVICE
London is a relatively safe city but before you travel, and while you're here, be sure to check out the latest safety advice.

www.gov.uk
All the latest information on security, health and local regulations from the UK Government.

www.met.police.uk
Information about major police incidents in the city.

www.relayuk.bt.com
App that helps those who are hearing- or speech-impaired contact 999 (emergency services) via SMS.

www.report-it.org.uk
A website for reporting hate crimes, with a list of organizations that can help victims.

ACCESSIBILITY
London is ranked as one of Europe's most accessible cities for anyone with mobility concerns. These resources will help make your journeys go smoothly.

www.euansguide.com
A forum for disabled access reviews on restaurants, theatres and attractions, by and for people with specific requirements.

www.scope.org.uk
Charity providing advice and support on how to get help on public transport.

www.tfl.gov.uk/transport-accessibility
Transport for London's official website with an accessible journey planner and up-to-date news on step-free station access.

www.visitlondon.com
London's official visitor guide with an Accessible London section, packed with tips on accessible hotels, tours and sights.

INDEX

ACKNOWLEDGMENTS

Meet the illustrator

*Award-winning British illustrator
David Doran is based in a studio by the
sea in Falmouth, Cornwall. When not
drawing and designing, David tries to make
the most of the beautiful area in which
he's based; sea-swimming all year round,
running the coastal paths and generally
spending as much time outside as possible.*

With thanks

*DK Eyewitness would like to thank the
following people for their contribution
to the first edition of this book: Florence
Derrick, Marlene Landu, Olivia Pass,
Lucy Richards, Tania Gomes, Zoë Rutland
and Casper Morris.*

This book was made with Forest Stewardship Council™ certified paper – one small step in DK's commitment to a sustainable future. **For more information go to www.dk.com/our-green-pledge**

A NOTE FROM DK EYEWITNESS

The world is fast-changing and it's keeping us folk at DK Eyewitness on our toes. We've worked hard to ensure that this edition of London Like a Local is up-to-date and reflects today's favourite places but we know that standards shift, venues close and new ones pop up in their place. So, if you notice something has closed, we've got something wrong or left something out, we want to hear about it. Please drop us a line at travelguides@dk.com

---

THIS EDITION UPDATED BY

Contributors Florence Derrick,
Zoë Rutland, Lucy Sara-Kelly, Bella Talbot
Senior Editor Lucy Richards
Senior Designer Stuti Tiwari
Designer Jordan Lambley
Indexer Helen Peters
Senior Cartographic Editor Casper Morris
Cartography Manager Suresh Kumar
Jacket Designer Sarah Snelling
Jacket Illustrator David Doran
Senior DTP Designer Tanveer Zaidi
Senior Production Editor Jason Little
Senior Production Controller Samantha Cross
Managing Editor Hollie Teague
Managing Art Editors Sarah Snelling, Priyanka Thakur
Art Director Maxine Pedliham
Publishing Director Georgina Dee

First edition 2021

Published in Great Britain by Dorling Kindersley Limited,
DK, One Embassy Gardens, 8 Viaduct Gardens,
London SW11 7BW.

The authorised representative in the EEA is
Dorling Kindersley Verlag GmbH. Arnulfstr. 124,
80636 Munich, Germany.

Published in the United States by DK Publishing,
1745 Broadway, 20th Floor, New York, NY 10019.

Copyright © 2021, 2023 Dorling Kindersley Limited
A Penguin Random House Company

22 23 24 25 10 9 8 7 6 5 4 3 2 1

The publishers cannot accept responsibility for any consequences arising from
the use of this book, nor for any material on third party websites, and cannot
guarantee that any website address in this book will be a suitable source of
travel information.

A CIP catalog record for this book is available from the British Library.

A catalog record for this book is available from the Library of Congress.

ISSN: 1542 1554
ISBN: 978 0 2415 6902 3

Printed and bound in China.

www.dk.com